Immigration Emergency Procedures

Immigration Emergency Procedures

Laurie Fransman, barrister
and
David Webb

Published by the Legal Action Group
March 1986

Laurie Fransman is an immigration barrister practising both at the Bar and at Tower Hamlets Law Centre. A writer and broadcaster on immigration and nationality law, he is the author of *British Nationality Law and the 1981 Act* second edition (Fourmat 1986) and the immigration author of *Tribunals Practice and Procedure* (Legal Studies & Services and Hemstal Press 1985). He is UK Contributing Editor of the United States publication *Immigration Law and Practice Reporter* (Matthew Bender, New York City, 1985) and co-author of *Immigration Law: Coming to the United Kingdom for Employment and Investment* (Fourmat, Autumn 1986). Laurie Fransman co-founded the Immigration Law Practitioners' Association and is now an executive member of that association.

David Webb is an immigration adviser at Tower Hamlets Law Centre, where he specialises in advocacy before the immigration appellate authorities. He is an executive member of the Immigration Law Practitioners' Association, on whose behalf he recently prepared a training course and manual on the rules relating to "secondary immigration". In 1984 he travelled to Bangladesh in order to investigate family settlement applications. He is a contributor to *Immigration Law and Practice* (Frank Cass Publications).

Phototypeset by Kerrypress Ltd, Luton, Beds
Printed by Dotesios (Printers) Ltd, Bradford-on-Avon, Wilts
ISSN 0307-3483
ISBN 0 905099 11 7

Acknowledgements

The authors would like to thank Roberta McDonald for her helpful comments on the manuscript.

Thanks are also due to the Immigration and Nationality Department for permission to reproduce the forms in Appendix 1, and to Her Majesty's Stationery Office for permission to reproduce the Immigration Act 1971.

The law is stated for England and Wales at 16 January 1986.

Contents

Table of Statutes

Table of Statutory Instruments

Table of Immigration Rules

The immigration rules are called "Statement of Changes in Immigration Rules (HC 169)". The current rules have been amended three times since coming into force in February 1983 (see further p7).

Table of Cases

Chapter One

Introduction

The purpose of this book is to assist the reader in dealing with an immigration emergency which requires immediate action. That action may be aimed at preventing the client's imminent removal from the UK and/or securing their release from detention. This book is not concerned with substantive immigration law or with the formal procedures whereby the decisions of the immigration authorities may be challenged. Both those subjects are more than adequately covered by existing texts (see appendix 3).

In order to cope with immigration emergencies one need neither be a lawyer nor well-versed in immigration law. Of course, a working knowledge of the system of immigration control is helpful, as is a basic understanding of the government department exercising that control. Accordingly, these matters are discussed in outline in chapter 2.

The approach to be adopted when faced with a potential emergency is essentially standard and a matter of common-sense. From the moment of first contact every effort must be made to ascertain the material facts and identify the problem. (This approach is discussed in greater detail in chapter 3.) Once the exact problem is known it will be clear whether or not an emergency exists. If there is no emergency (for example the client will not be removed because s/he has an appeal pending), there will be sufficient time in which to pass the case to an immigration practitioner or agency. However, where there is a serious degree of urgency, the problem must be classified (see chapter 4) and the appropriate procedures for dealing with that emergency must be applied (see chapters 4 and 5). The task, generally, is to avert the imminent danger and gain control of the case. That task will be assisted by the various appendices at the end of the book.

Chapter Two

Law and Administrative Structure

2.1 The Immigration Act 1971 and the Immigration Rules

Immigration law seeks to define those who may enter and/or remain in the UK and the terms upon which they may do so. The details are set out in the Immigration Act 1971 and the "Immigration Rules" (see further below); the Act provides the basic scheme of immigration control and is complemented by the Rules which refer to specific categories of persons.

All statutory references refer to the Immigration Act 1971 unless otherwise stated.

2.2 The right of abode

(a) Generally

Persons with the right of abode in the UK are not subject to immigration control (s1(1)). All others require "permission" to enter or remain (s1(2)). Every British citizen has the right of abode (irrespective of how that status was acquired) as do certain Commonwealth citizens (s2 as amended by the British Nationality Act 1981 s39(2)). Commonwealth citizens who have the right of abode are those who by 1 January 1983 (when the 1981 Act came into force) qualified as patrials under the *old* s2 (ie before it was amended by the 1981 Act). The standard texts on immigration and nationality (set out in appendix 3) discuss this area of law. Suffice it here to say all persons who automatically became British citizens on 1 January 1983 will, so long as they are still British citizens, have the right of abode in the UK. All Commonwealth citizens who by that date acquired patriality will also, so long as they are still Commonwealth citizens, have the right of abode. Persons who since 1 January 1983 have become British citizens will, of course, also have the right of abode. However, since that date it has been impossible for any Commonwealth citizen to acquire the right of abode as a separate immigration status. The 1981 Act, by amending s2, ensures that the right of abode may now be acquired only by the acquisition of British citizenship itself. The right of abode as a separate status now exists only in respect of those Commonwealth citizens who acquired it before the new law came into force. When that generation passes on, the right of abode will be no more than a feature of British citizenship itself.

(b) Relevance to port emergencies

The right of abode may well be relevant when an emergency arises. Experience shows that a significant number of passengers involved in port emergencies actually have a claim to the right of abode. The critical distinction is that while some of these passengers are required to prove that claim *prior* to arrival at a UK port of entry, others do not. Further, those who may claim the right of abode upon arrival will have a right of appeal against any refusal of the claim and may *remain in the UK* while they exercise that right. Astonishingly, this procedure is little known and little used. The case examples on pp5–6 illustrate the need for persons dealing with immigration emergencies to have a working knowledge of the substantive law involved.

(c) Claiming the right of abode upon arrival

Persons who may claim the right of abode upon arrival and who may appeal from within the UK if the claim is rejected, are not clearly identified in the Act. The right of appeal is given by s13(1), but it is qualified by s13(3), which refers to s3(9) which, in turn, refers to the old s2. The effect of this complex of law is that only *certain* persons who claim to be *British citizens* may claim the right of abode upon arrival. Commonwealth citizens who claim the right of abode but who do not claim also to be British citizens have to prove their claim *before* travelling to the UK by obtaining a "certificate of entitlement".

The persons who claim to be British citizens and who need make that claim only upon arrival, include, it is submitted, the following:

(i) *British by birth* A passenger who is British because s/he was born in the UK does not have to prove that fact before arriving at a port of entry. Of course, if a British passport has been obtained, no problem will arise. However, if the passenger is travelling on some other passport, entry may be refused (see case example (A), below).

(ii) *British by descent* A person who on the face of it is British by descent does not need to prove a claim to the right of abode before travelling to the UK. There are presently thousands of young persons outside the UK who wish to come here, and who are entitled to do so, but they do not know the law. Many of the men who have come to the UK from the Indian sub-continent since the second world war are now British citizens by having been registered or naturalised here. The wives and children of these men represent the greatest source of secondary immigration to the UK. The wait for an initial "entry clearance" interview at British posts in India, Pakistan and Bangladesh may be two years or more. Indeed, the Home Office relies, it appears, on these delays as a means of regulating the flow of these women and children into the UK (*Guardian* 21 March 1985 p2). The belief on the sub-continent is that even where the husband/father is British, permission must always be obtained before travelling to the UK. Regarding wives, this is true in that at best they have a claim to the right of abode but not to British citizenship itself, and so must obtain a certificate of entitlement before travelling. *However, the children who on the face of it are British citizens by descent may travel direct to the UK and, if refused entry, may appeal without having to leave.* They do not require entry clearance. On this point, one is advised to read *Momotaj Begum (Parvin)* (4280) unreported.

With certain limited exceptions, British posts overseas insist on processing the wives and children of British men as persons who are subject to immigration control (ie having no apparent claim to the right of abode); Home Office letter to Tower Hamlets Law Centre dated 6 February 1984. (See, further, *Kessori Khatun* (4272) unreported.) Thus, the application of the law is largely limited to port emergencies, in that the majority of aircraft arriving from the sub-continent probably have among their passengers persons who could claim to have the right of abode and who could appeal from within the UK were that claim to be rejected (see case example B, below).

(iii) *Certain British women* Certain women who are not from the UK and who are not British by descent may nevertheless claim to be British citizens without the need to establish that claim prior to arrival. As the law is complicated (and the group to which it applies small) suffice it simply to state that this category exists.

(d) The need to consider whether a claim exists

The first (and probably most important) question to consider in any immigration case is whether or not the client has a claim to the right of abode. This applies to port emergencies as much as to any other area and, for this reason, the suggested questionnaire at appendix 4 is designed to elicit the relevant facts.

There are two reasons why, in an emergency, the question must be considered. First, a passenger is sometimes better advised to leave the UK rather than languish in detention for several weeks, for example, the passenger's case may be completely hopeless and his or her eventual removal from the UK inevitable (see further chapter 4.1). This is probably the only aspect of emergency procedures that requires some consideration of the *merits* of the client's case and, in giving that consideration, the issue of the right of abode should be borne in mind.

Second, contact with the port immigration authorities will seldom reveal that a possible claim to the right of abode is involved. Theoretically, two decisions have to be made in respect of each and every passenger seeking to enter the UK: "does this passenger require leave to enter?" and, if so, "should leave be granted?". A passenger who has a claim to the right of abode, which claim need *not* be proved before travelling to the UK, does *not* require "leave to enter" (ss1(1) and 3(1)). In practice, unless a passenger produces a British passport or expressly claims not to require leave in that s/he has the right of abode, the immigration officer will *assume* that leave is required. Indeed, in these circumstances the passenger need not formally be notified of the decision that leave to enter is required (Immigration Appeals (Notices) Regulations 1984 SI No 2040 reg 3(5)). So where, for example, the passenger is a child who has a claim to British citizenship by descent, the notice refusing that child entry will state only that leave to enter has been refused (for whatever reason) and that the passenger may appeal against that refusal but only from *outside* the UK.

Accordingly, it rests wholly upon the person handling the emergency to consider and to raise, if relevant, the issue of the right of abode.

(e) Raising the issue of the right of abode

Where it appears that the passenger *may* have a claim to the right of abode, which need not be proved before travelling to the UK, if time is of the essence the port immigration authorities should be contacted immediately. Invariably, one will be referred to a duty chief immigration officer (CIO). It should then be explained that the passenger is contesting the decision that *leave to enter is required* in that, by virtue of s13(1), a right of appeal exists against that decision which, by virtue of s13(3), may be exercised prior to removal. Further, that, if it is the view of the immigration authorities that no such right exists, the question will be taken to the High Court by way of a judicial review.

Usually, even the threat of judicial review will not be necessary (assuming that the passenger has correctly been identified as one whose claim may be made on arrival). In any event, though, such an approach is bound to delay the passenger's removal from the UK long enough, at least, for expert advice to be obtained. The emergency will have passed.

(f) Case examples

The following two cases illustrate law and procedure. For further information see the texts set out in appendix 3.

CASE EXAMPLE A

P was born in the UK. When aged two, he was taken to India with his parents for an extended holiday. While there, his British passport was lost. He applied to the British High Commission for a new passport, producing his birth certificate. The High Commission was not satisfied that P was the person whose name appeared on that birth certificate. After many months his father brought him to the UK on an Indian passport and without any sort of prior permission from the High Commission. The port emergency that resulted was dealt with on the basis that P had a right of abode in the UK and needed to prove that right only on arrival. Having the right of abode, he did not require leave to enter and any decision to the contrary would be appealable within the UK. After considering the evidence, it was agreed that P was born here and therefore a British citizen.

CASE EXAMPLE B

A, his mother, brothers and sisters all applied to the British High Commission in Bangladesh for permission to join their husband/father in the UK. A's application was refused although all the rest were granted "entry certificates". A, now five years old, was nevertheless brought to the UK by his family. A was born in Bangladesh in 1979, by which time his father had become British by registering in the UK. At Heathrow, as no express application was made to the contrary, it was assumed that A was subject to immigration control and so required leave to enter. Not having obtained an entry certificate, he was therefore refused leave and arrangements were made for his removal back to Bangladesh. In dealing with this emergency, the CIO on duty at terminal three was told that A contested the (implicit) decision that he required leave to enter. The CIO readily agreed that, on the face of it, A did not require leave and that he would have a right of appeal prior to removal if it was decided otherwise. Despite the decision to refuse leave, the CIO re-opened the case and requested evidence in support of A's claim to the right of abode.

2.3 The control of those with no right of abode

(a) The Immigration Act's scheme of control

Having stated that persons with the right of abode are not subject to immigration control (s1(1)), the Act goes on to say that all others require "permission" to enter and/or remain in the UK. This permission is known as "leave": leave to *enter* is given by "immigration officers" at the port of entry (s4(1)); leave to *remain* is given by the Secretary of State, after entry (s4(1)). Leave (to enter or remain) may be for a limited or an indefinite period (s3(1)(b)). Leave given for only a limited period may be made subject to conditions restricting employment and/or requiring registration with the police (s3(1)(c)). Limited leave and the conditions attached to it may be varied in different ways and if it is changed to indefinite leave, all conditions will be lifted (s3(3)(a)).

Whether a person has indefinite leave, limited leave or no leave, if s/he is subject to immigration control s/he can be deported (s3(5), (6); but see s7). During the currency of a deportation order it is impossible to possess valid leave (s5(1)).

Any person subject to a deportation order is liable to be detained pending removal from the UK (s5(5) and Sch 3). Illegal entrants and passengers refused leave to enter are also liable to be detained pending removal from the UK (s4(2)(c) and (d) and Sch 2).

The Act provides that the Secretary of State may from time to time lay "statements of rules" before Parliament and that those rules may contain all the necessary details in relation to the various groups of persons in respect of whom the powers to grant leave etc may be exercised (s3(2)). The Act itself says no more than that the rules must provide for "persons coming for the purpose of taking employment, or for purposes of study, or as visitors, or as dependants . . ." (s1(4)). The current rules are called "Statement of Changes in Immigration Rules (HC 169)" and are referred to simply as the "Immigration Rules".

(b) The Immigration Rules (HC 169)

Although the Rules are not "law" in the same way as a statute, but rather guidance to applicants and to the immigration authorities, for the purposes of immigration proceedings generally they are to be seen as having the *force* of law (*R v Secretary of State for the Home Department ex parte Hosenball* [1977] 3 All ER 452, CA). Since the current Rules (HC 169) came into force in February 1983, they have been amended three times. In April 1985 HC 293 amended the provisions relating to doctors and dentists; in May 1985 the Appendix was varied by Cmnd 9539 to include Sri Lankans in the list of visa nationals; and in July/August 1985 a variety of substantial changes were made by HC 503. All references in this book to paragraphs within HC 169 are references to those paragraphs *as originally numbered.*

In respect of various categories of persons (such as visitors and artists) the Rules state the circumstances in which, and terms upon which, leave to enter (section one) and leave to remain (section two) may be granted.

The Rules also provide that, in addition to leave to enter, some passengers must obtain "entry clearance" before travelling to the UK (HC 169 paras 10–14). A holder of prior entry clearance may still be refused leave to enter, but only on limited grounds (see para 13) and even then a right of appeal (at least against the applicability of para 13) may be exercised immediately from within the UK (s13(3)).

An entry clearance will take one of three forms: a "visa" for visa nationals (see Appendix to HC 169); a "Home Office Letter of Consent" (for other foreign nationals); and an "entry certificate" (for most Commonwealth citizens). Visa nationals will require a visa *irrespective* of the purpose for which they seek entry. Other foreign nationals and most Commonwealth citizens will require entry clearance only when seeking entry for *certain* purposes. (A "certificate of entitlement" is very different from an entry clearance—although it is also obtained before travelling, it is proof of one's right of abode in the UK.)

Where a given individual does not fall within any of the categories listed in the Rules, or where s/he cannot satisfy one or more of the conditions, as the Secretary of State has a power to act outside the Rules (see *R v IAT ex parte Firat* (1983) 12 January 1983 (unreported), QBD; *R v IAT ex parte Wirdestedt* (1984) *Times* 15 February, DC), it is always open to an individual to request the Secretary of State to exercise his discretion and grant leave exceptionally. The principal method by which the Secretary of State is requested to grant leave despite the scope and requirements of the Rules is referred to as "the making of representations". In the context of emergency procedures, representations are often used and sometimes successful. They are considered further in chapter 5.3, below.

Administrative Structure

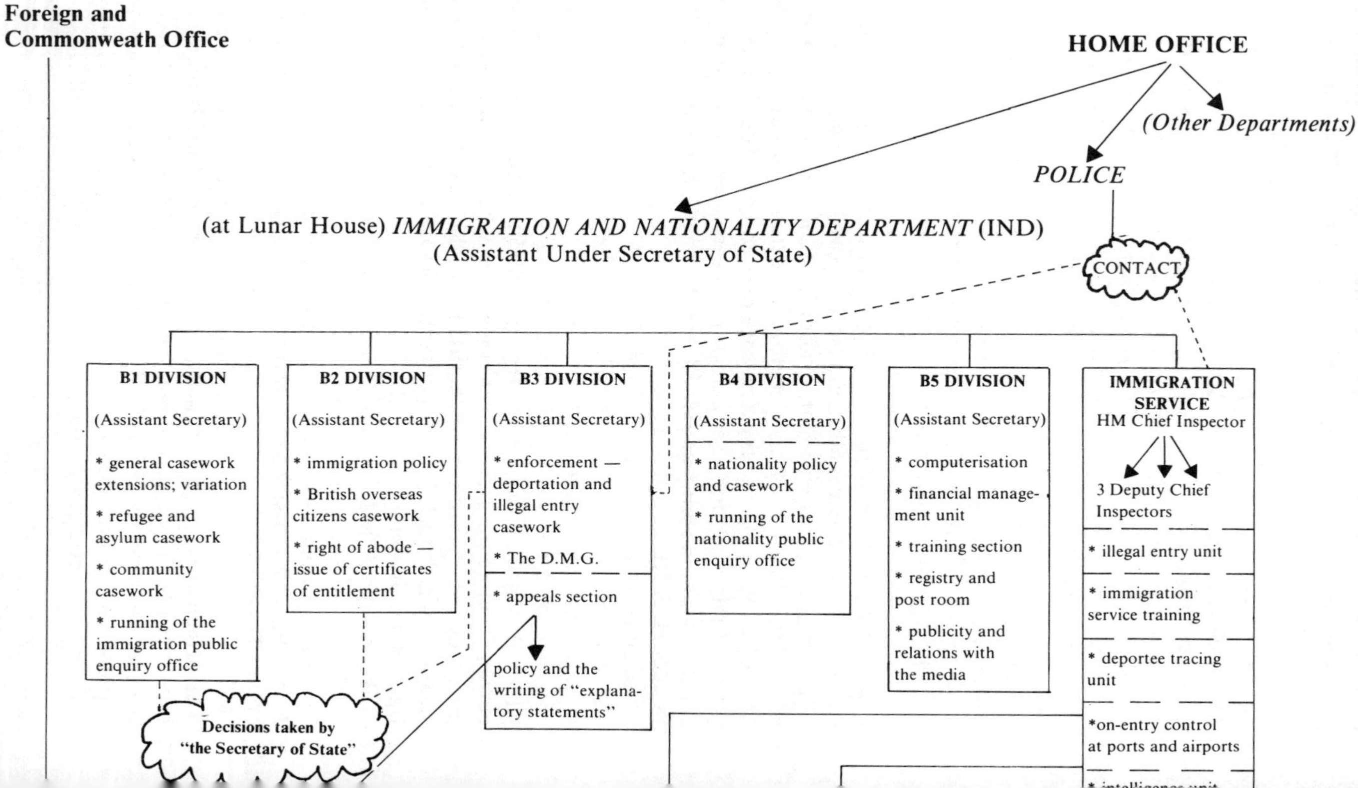

central London and Harmondsworth | Leeds | Manchester | Birmingham

Ports of Entry

Heathrow Terminals 1 & 2	Heathrow Terminal 3	Gatwick	other ports fall into districts (eg the South East)
(Asst. Chief Inspector)	(Asst. Chief Inspector)	(Asst. Chief Inspector)	(Asst. Chief Inspector)
(Inspectors)	(Inspectors)	(Inspectors)	(Inspectors)
(CIOs)	(CIOs)	(CIOs)	(CIOs)
(IOs)	(IOs)	(IOs)	(IOs)

two principal units divide London on the bases of Metropolitan police districts

British posts abroad — FCO runs them. Staffed by entry clearance officers from FCO and on secondment from the Home Office.

Decisions taken by "an immigration officer"

Decisions taken by "an entry clearance officer"

2.4 Administrative structure (Immigration Service etc)

(a) Generally

The principal authority responsible for administration is the Immigration and Nationality Department (IND) of the Home Office. The IND is based in Croydon though the Ministers' private offices are in Queen Anne's Gate, London SW1. A basic understanding of the IND's structure is important for two reasons. Firstly, it can assist in identifying the nature of an emergency (for example, if Isis House is involved the problem is unlikely to involve a passenger seeking entry). Secondly, a knowledge of the system may assist in dealing with an emergency (for example, if a CIO will not grant temporary admission it may help to approach the inspector). The paragraphs that follow briefly consider some of the features of the IND that will be of interest to persons dealing with immigration emergencies. This structure is also explained by means of the diagrams on pp8 and 9.

(b) Passengers seeking entry

The control of persons seeking entry is in the hands of the Immigration Service. A chief inspector and three deputy chief inspectors head the Immigration Service. They are based in Lunar House (Croydon). Generally, the UK is divided into districts (for example, the south east) and each district is the responsibility of an assistant chief inspector. Additionally, Heathrow terminals 1 and 2 share an assistant chief inspector and another is responsible for terminal 3. At least one of these inspectors will be on duty between 8 am and 10 pm at Heathrow. An assistant chief inspector also sits at Gatwick, but again, 24-hour coverage is not available. At all ports of entry the majority of passengers are processed by immigration officers (IOs). When difficulties arise, though, a CIO will usually take over the case or, at least, be consulted. Immigration officers are empowered to grant or refuse leave to enter (see above). Their other powers (and port emergencies generally) are considered in chapter 4.1.

(c) Persons present in the UK

The Secretary of State is empowered to grant leave to remain and to vary leave in different ways (see 2.3 para *(a)*, above). The functions are generally carried out by B1 Division. Decisions of the Secretary of State which are *not* taken within B1 include decisions to grant or refuse a certificate of entitlement (to the right of abode) and decisions to make deportation orders. While the former is the responsibility of B2 Division, deportation decisions are taken within B3.

Regarding the tracing and detention of persons liable to removal as deportees or illegal entrants, the Immigration Service and B3 Division carry out different aspects of those activities. Preliminary investigative work is carried out by the Immigration Service, mainly through the offices of Isis House in Southwark and the Intelligence Unit at Harmondsworth. Of course, close links with the police have also been established. See also chapter 4.2, below.

(d) Persons outside the UK

Minor exceptions aside, entry clearance and certificate of entitlement applications (see 2.3 para *(b)*, above) are processed by the immigration and consular sections of British posts abroad. These are administered by the Foreign and Commonwealth Office, though IND officers on secondment from the Home Office will assist. Decisions are generally taken by entry clearance officers (some of whom may be referred to as visa officers). Fairly often entry clearance applications will be referred to the IND for a decision to be made. Such decisions will be taken within B1.

(e) Appeals

Any appealable decision, whether taken by an entry clearance officer, IO or the Secretary of State, must be formally notified in writing (Notice Regulations 1984 reg 3(1)) and the notice must explain how the right of appeal may be exercised (reg 4(1)(c)). Appeal proceedings are initiated by the giving of "notice of appeal" (Immigration Appeals (Procedure) Rules 1984 SI No 2041 r4). The case will ultimately come before an immigration appeal adjudicator (or the Immigration Appeal Tribunal (IAT)) at which time the respondent will be represented either by an officer attached to B3 Division or by an officer of the Immigration Service (usually a CIO).

The issue of appeals, insofar as it relates to emergency procedures, is discussed further in chapter 5.5, below.

Chapter Three

Dealing with Emergencies

3.1 Initial contact

A commonly held misconception is that dealing with immigration emergencies is an acquired art or skill, or just plain difficult. In reality, no "secret" is involved. On the contrary, the approach to be taken in both ascertaining and dealing with emergency situations is hardly more than the application of common-sense and is not really deserving of an entire chapter. As with all things, of course, an initial lack of confidence is inevitable, but this is soon dissipated by the familiarity brought by a little experience.

Dealing with emergencies requires neither legal qualification nor expertise in immigration law.

An immigration emergency will begin with a telephone call or personal visit. The caller or visitor may be the person whose problem it is, or may be a friend or relative (hereafter referred to as "the contact" for convenience). The client or his or her contact will explain that some sort of immigration problem exists and that help is required as a matter of urgency. In busy solicitors' firms, voluntary agencies and the like, there is always a temptation to deal with new cases by dispensing appointments rather than by listening. The necessity of this practice in non-urgent cases is recognised. Nevertheless, an enquirer should never be left with no more than an appointment unless and until it has been determined with certainty that immediate action is not required. When in doubt, or when satisfied that further enquiries must be made, one should be prepared to rearrange one's commitments accordingly. Although resolving an emergency may involve no more than a telephone call or two, it may (at the other extreme) require a couple of hours of telephone calls and interviews to be followed shortly by written representations.

3.2 Ascertaining the facts

As with any new matter the facts of the case must be ascertained before advice can be given or action considered. Firstly, as much relevant information as possible must be elicited from the client or contact. The questionnaire at appendix 4 is designed to do just this. In all common immigration emergencies this questionnaire, once completed, will provide the client's necessary personal details and family circumstances, and his or her likely immigration and nationality status. The questionnaire also asks for any port, Home Office, or other reference numbers as well as for any letters, forms, or notices recently issued to the client by the immigration authorities. Such documentation taken together with the completed questionnaire and the client's passport (if available) will provide at least a preliminary set of facts upon which to proceed. The following points are worth noting:

(a) *Questionnaire* Initially one should take the client or contact carefully and methodically through the entire questionnaire. After dealing with a few emergencies, though, the questionnaire will probably become just a simple check-list. Eventually, it may be abandoned altogether;

(b) *Documentation* A letter, form, or notice issued by an immigration authority will usually say a great deal about the client's predicament. These documents are, for the most part, self-explanatory. If in any doubt, though, appendix 1 may assist in identifying the document and in explaining its significance; and

(c) *Passport* The passport is, of course, an excellent source of information relating to the client's personal details and likely immigration and nationality status. However, rubber-stamp endorsements are not nearly as self-explanatory as the documentation referred to above. "Reading" a passport may help to determine any previous immigration status possessed by the client as well as his or her probable current status. Accordingly, appendix 3 refers to two immigration texts which set out the various endorsements, their meaning and significance and reference is also made to a *LAG Bulletin* article which deals with that material succinctly and conveniently.

The stage has been reached at which as much relevant information as possible has been obtained through the questionnaire, documentation and passport. A word of caution, though: the client or contact will occasionally omit crucial facts or misstate them, and will often use precise legal terms at random. One should guard against these dangers, particularly when contacting the appropriate immigration authority (see chapter 3.4, below).

A preliminary assessment of the available facts can now be made.

3.3 Identifying the problem

Bearing in mind that the purpose of this chapter is to advise one how to act when urgent action is required, the initial question must be "is this an emergency?". An "emergency" can be defined in different ways, but as explained in chapter 1, above, here we are proceeding on the basis that an "emergency" will be limited to a situation demanding immediate action; that is to say, one which leaves no time in which to obtain expert advice or refer the case to an immigration practitioner or specialist agency.

The information obtained through the questionnaire, documentation and passport (see 3.2, above) will allow one, as a matter of fact, to identify the problem as one of the following:

(a) the client will have sought to enter the UK. Enquiries may still be under way or entry may already have been formally refused. The client may or may not be in detention.

Generally, this is referred to as a port emergency and is considered further in chapter 4.1, below;

(b) the client will have entered the UK some time in the past. The police and/or immigration authorities have arrested him or her or are looking for him or her.

This sort of emergency generally involves the (threatened) arrest and detention of a person who has no permission to be in the UK. The person may be *liable to immediate removal* as an illegal entrant or deportee (see chapter 4.2, below). On the other hand, if the client appears to have entered the country legally and is not subject to a current deportation order, then the problem will usually be that s/he is an overstayer (ie has remained longer than allowed to) or is wanted for some other immigration offence (see chapter 4.3);

(c) the client's only problem, or additional problem, may simply be that s/he appears to have a right of appeal against some decision or action made or taken by an immigration authority or an appellate authority, but the deadline for bringing an appeal has just about passed.

This is a "time limit" problem. Although such problems are usually solved easily and quickly, they are nevertheless emergencies which, if left unattended, will have serious consequences. Such problems are considered further in chapter 4.4, below;

(d) the client's only (or additional) problem may be that s/he is experiencing financial distress pending the outcome of an application, appeal or emergency procedure.

Such financial emergencies are discussed in chapter 4.5, below; or

(e) finally, the position may simply be that the client *could* fall within (b), above, but is considering pre-empting such an emergency by voluntarily approaching the immigration authorities in the hope of "regularising" his or her status.

The causes of emergencies are looked at further in chapter 4.6, below.

3.4 Dealing with the problem

As a general rule, the first step towards dealing with an emergency will be to contact the appropriate immigration authority. The facts of the case will indicate which authority is appropriate and telephone numbers and addresses are provided in appendix 2.

The initial aim of any conversation with the immigration authorities should always be to confirm the facts that have been obtained through the questionnaire, documentation and passport (see 3.2, above). To do otherwise may result in having to consume a vast quantity of humble pie and so put one at a distinct disadvantage. If the facts (and the problem arising from them) turn out to be quite different from those originally ascertained, the immigration authority should be given no more than one's name and telephone number and the expectation of further contact once instructions have been taken. The client must then be re-interviewed and a fresh assessment made.

Apart from confirming the relevant facts, the purpose of contacting the appropriate authority will usually be to *inform* it of procedures to be employed and/or to *request* it to do something. For example, in a given case one may inform the immigration office at Heathrow terminal 3 that a Member of Parliament is to obtain a stop order (so that representations may be made) and that, therefore, an extension of temporary admission is requested.

To be properly equipped to deal with an emergency one must know of the procedures at one's disposal. These are contained in chapter 5, below. There, the use of each procedure is explained as is the method by which to apply the procedure. *When* each procedure should be used is explained in chapter 4.

Chapter Four

Principal Emergency Situations

4.1 Emergencies at port of entry

(a) Introduction
All passengers subject to immigration control are required to submit to examination on arrival at a port of entry. "Port emergencies" arise when a person is seeking entry to the UK but the authorities doubt his or her eligibility to do so under the Immigration Act 1971 and the Immigration Rules.

The different factual situations with which one may be faced are categorised at 4.1 para *(f)*, below. First, however, if one is to act in this field it is essential to have at least a working knowledge of the law and practice relating to "port refusals". Anyone without some grounding in the subject will find it hard to understand the terminology of the forms and the language of IOs and will be unable fully to appreciate the situation much less be able to deal with any emergency that may already exist, or be rapidly developing. Accordingly, the procedures adopted by IOs when examining passengers, and the grounds given for refusing leave, are outlined below. It is stressed that the information given is not intended to be a comprehensive statement of the substantive law: the details of the Rules and the relevant caselaw can of course be researched more fully in the existing texts mentioned at appendix 3.

(b) The examination
Schedule 2 of the Immigration Act states what actions IOs can take in carrying out their duties. It should be stressed that they have very extensive powers, several (but not all) of which are mentioned below. Of course, the Act does not go into minute detail as regards the procedure that IO's should adopt. Schedule 2 para 1(3) simply states that in exercising their functions IOs shall act in accordance with "instructions" not inconsistent with the Immigration Rules, as may be given to them by the Secretary of State. These "Secret Instructions" are a constant source of reference for officials.

Although every person subject to immigration control is liable to examination, in practice an IO has to decide quickly whether a particular person should be examined in depth. To quote a pasage from a Home Office note entitled "Discrimination in the Immigration Control", recently submitted to the CRE:

> "Such decisions have to be made at a stage when the available evidence may be meagre—usually a passport, the answers to a couple of questions and a passenger's appearance and demeanour. . . . Experience of the categories of passenger from whom evasion has most commonly been detected in the past is bound to influence the IO as to the passengers he selects for closer examination."

The "couple of questions" will be an IO enquiring about the purpose and intended duration of the proposed stay in the UK.

If, from the answers to these questions, the IO has doubts as to whether the relevant Immigration Rules can be met (see 4.1 para *(c)*, below), a more intensive examination will be conducted. It should be noted that an IO has the power to detain a person pending his or her examination (Sch 2 para 16(1)). In some ports the same IO conducts the initial and further examinations, in other places there are different interviewers employed at different times. Passengers required to submit to further examination will usually be issued with Form IS81 (see appendix 1 group A). Precisely when this form is issued varies but it will normally be given after the IO has ended a round of questioning but still feels unable to reach a decision without making further enquiries.

The authorities use the IS81 notice because Sch 2 para 6(1) states that an IO must give a decision to grant or refuse leave not later than 12 hours after the conclusion of his or her examination (including any further examination), and that, if this is not done, the person is deemed to have been given indefinite leave to enter. Therefore, by serving IS81 on a passenger the IO makes it clear for the record that the examination is not yet completed and that the 12-hour period has not started to run.

An IO has the right to ask a person whether s/he is carrying or conveying documents of any description specified: for example, the IO can ask whether s/he has any letters from the family s/he intends to visit, or correspondence from the college in which s/he intends to study (Sch 2 para 4(2)). After having asked the person about documents s/he possesses, an IO (or another acting under his or her directions) can search that person and any baggage belonging to him or her. This is a regular practice. There is a proviso that women must be searched only by their own sex.

As it is up to the passenger to show that s/he is eligible for admission, lack of co-operation with the immigration authorities will almost invariably lead to a refusal of leave to enter. Indeed, s26(1), which lists criminal offences capable of arising from the administration of the Immigration Act, states that refusing or failing to submit to an examination or to produce information/documents to an IO is punishable on summary conviction with a £200 fine and/or six months' imprisonment.

Detailed interrogation may last several hours. If a passenger is being met by relatives or friends, these people will generally also be invited to the "secondary examination" area, and very often will themselves be questioned. For example, where there is intensive examination of a person seeking entry as a visitor the sponsor, if present to meet him or her, is likely to be requested to answer questions about him or herself and the would-be entrant. Any "discrepancies" that arise will be said to affect the passenger's "credibility"—a matter on which IOs place great stress.

It should be borne in mind that although an IO is an administrative and not a judicial officer, s/he must nevertheless act honestly and fairly and in accordance with natural justice (see *Mughal* [1973] 3 All ER 796). However, in all but extreme cases the courts are most reluctant to intervene in "port emergency" situations.

Finally, it should be mentioned that quite frequently the immigration authorities defer a decision pending the outcome of further enquiries (for example, contacting the Home Office in Croydon to seek information about previous periods of stay, or telexing British Embassies/High Commissions abroad to establish what a passenger stated when applying for entry clearance). The information sought is often not immediately forthcoming, and so the person will be either detained (at Harmondsworth Detention Centre, for example) or, as is more usual, granted "temporary admission". The concept and use of temporary admission is fully considered in chapter 5.2 below.

(c) Grounds for refusing leave

There are various grounds on which admission may be refused:

(i) technical reasons such as the lack of a necessary travel document or mandatory entry clearance;

(ii) the finding that, although entry clearance was obtained, it is ineffective because either it was obtained by deception or circumstances have changed since its issue;

(iii) the finding that a person who arrives without entry clearance (in circumstances in which it is optional) does not meet the requirements of the Immigration Rules for the specific category in which entry is sought;

(iv) refusal on one of the "general" grounds laid down by the Immigration Rules.

These grounds for refusal will be considered briefly in turn.

(i) *Refusing leave to enter due to the lack of necessary documentation*

Admission to the UK requires various types of documentation to be produced by the would-be entrant. All passengers on arrival must produce a passport or equivalent document which is acceptable to the authorities. Obviously, entry can be refused if the authorities believe the documentation to be forged or the passenger to be impersonating the person named. As explained in chapter 2.3, above, some persons are also required to produce a valid entry clearance. Furthermore, persons (other than EEC nationals) who are coming to take employment must hold a work permit.

"Visa nationals" who arrive at a port of entry without a passport endorsed with a current UK visa may be refused leave to enter on that ground alone. (It should be emphasised that a work permit is *not* an entry clearance, and so visa nationals holding such permits must also produce a current visa on arrival.)

As regards non-visa nationals (except EEC nationals), entry clearance is mandatory if seeking admission for the purpose of:

(a) permit-free employment (ministers of religion, representatives of overseas firms, etc) (HC 169 paras 31–34);
(b) establishing oneself in business or self-employment (HC 169 paras 35–37);
(c) entry as a person of independent means (HC 169 para 38);
(d) entry as a writer or artist (HC 169 para 39); or
(e) settlement as a dependent fiance(e), spouse or child of a person settled in the UK (HC 503 paras 8–12, amending HC 169 paras 41–50).

Therefore, if a person arrives seeking entry under a category for which entry clearance was required but not obtained, then again a port emergency can arise.

Entry clearance is *not* mandatory for non-visa nationals who seek leave to enter as:

(a) visitors (HC 169 paras 17–20);
(b) students (HC 169 paras 21–25); or
(c) Commonwealth citizens aged between 17–27 who are coming for an extended holiday (HC 169 para 30).

Nevertheless, many people (particularly those from new Commonwealth countries) for whom technically entry clearance is not required do apply to a British High Commission or Embassy for (optional) clearance before they travel. This practice is generally encouraged by the authorities who argue that possession of such clearance indicates that an entry clearance officer has previously considered the matter and been satisfied, thus preventing delays and difficulties at the port of entry.

(ii) *Refusing leave to enter to persons who hold entry clearance* The fact that a person possesses valid entry clearance does *not* mean that s/he will be admitted automatically. Every passenger subject to immigration control is required to submit to examination by an IO irrespective of whether that person has entry clearance. However, para 13 of the Immigration Rules states that a passenger who does hold current entry clearance is not to be refused leave to enter unless the IO is satisfied that:

(a) false representations were employed or material facts not disclosed (whether orally or in writing and whether or not to the passenger's knowledge) for the purpose of obtaining that clearance; or
(b) a change in circumstances since clearance was issued has removed the basis of the holder's claim for admission; or
(c) one of the "general" grounds justifying refusal is established. (As regards this last point see (iv), below.)

There are numerous cases considering para 13, but a discussion of what amounts to material facts not disclosed or a change in circumstances is outside the scope of this book. Suffice it to say that the onus of proof is on the authorities to establish their case, and that the recent case of *Kwabena* (1985) *Times* 28 May is relevant.

Persons who arrive with clearance and who are then refused leave are *not* in the typical "port emergency" situation. This is because they are allowed to remain in the UK while exercising their right of appeal against refusal (s13(3)). However, the appropriate appeal forms (see appendix 1 group F) should of course be lodged immediately.

(iii) *Refusing leave to enter to persons who do not meet the specific immigration rules for the category in which entry is sought* If a non-visa national arrives without entry clearance and seeks leave to enter under a category for which prior clearance is not mandatory, leave will be granted only if the would-be entrant meets the specific requirements laid down for that category (for example, a would-be visitor must establish that s/he is genuinely seeking entry for the period of the visit, that s/he will be maintained and accommodated without recourse to public funds, and that s/he can meet the cost of the return or onward journey). If such persons are refused leave to enter, they have a right of appeal to an adjudicator against that refusal (s13(1)). However, this right of appeal is exercisable only after they have *left* the UK (s13(3)). Removal is therefore imminent and the emergency must be dealt with in other ways, which are detailed in later chapters.

It is clear that if a non-visa national arrives at a port holding entry clearance found to be ineffective by virtue of para 13 (see (ii) above), the IO should then go on to consider the fresh representations of the applicant as to whether s/he can meet the requirements of the Rules relevant to the category for which s/he seeks entry. It is now settled that there is a right of appeal, exercisable *before* removal from the UK, against not only the refusal to admit him or her by virtue of his or her entry clearance, but also, the entry clearance having proved to be ineffective, against refusal to admit because s/he does not otherwise qualify for entry under the Rules (see *Chanda* [1981] Imm AR 88).

(iv) *Refusing leave to enter on a "general" ground* A passenger may satisfy the formal requirements of a specific immigration "category" and yet be refused entry on the grounds of:

(a) "restricted returnability", ie failing to satisfy an IO that s/he will be admitted to another country after a stay in the UK (HC 169 para 15);
(b) for medical reasons (HC 169 paras 79–82);
(c) through having a criminal record (HC 169 para 83);
(d) because the passenger is subject to a deportation order (HC 169 para 83); or
(e) because exclusion is conducive to the public good (HC 169 para 85).

Paragraph 76, in expressly stating that the fact that a person satisfies the formal requirements of a specific category is not conclusive in his or her favour, gives examples of where leave to enter may be refused. In particular it states that a person may be refused leave to enter on the ground that s/he has not observed time limits or conditions imposed on any previous grant of leave to enter or remain. (However, although a person who holds a current entry clearance can be refused entry on the grounds described above, for example, restricted returnability, exclusion conducive to the public good etc, such a person should not be refused on the ground of previous breaches of immigration law unless there was non-disclosure or false representations were made by the applicant about his or her immigration history in obtaining such clearance).

It should be noted that a "returning resident" who was a Commonwealth citizen settled in the UK on 1 January 1973, or the wife or child under 18 (holding valid "settlement" entry clearance) of a Commonwealth citizen settled in the UK on that date, can be refused leave to enter only on the ground that s/he is currently subject to a deportation order (HC 169 para 77).

There is no right of appeal against refusal of leave to enter on the ground of exclusion for the public good if the direction to refuse entry was personally given by the Secretary of State as opposed to an IO (s13(5); see Form IS82B at appendix 1 group A). As regards refusals under the other "general" grounds, although there is a right of appeal, unless the passenger is in possession of a current entry clearance the right is of little immediate assistance for the reasons explained above.

(d) The decision

It should be appreciated that IOs retain and exercise considerable *discretion* both within and outside the Rules to admit persons who apparently fall short of the requirements. The question of discretion will be raised again in chapter 5.3 below, in relation to the value of "representations".

Although an IO can grant leave to enter, the approval of a CIO or an immigration inspector must always be obtained if leave is to be refused (HC 169 para 78). Furthermore, the passenger should be handed a written notice (see appendix 1 group A) informing him of the decision and of the reasons for refusal (HC 169 para 89). This notice, which should be explained if the passenger has difficulty in understanding its wording, should also explain the right of appeal (if one exists) against the decision. As has been stated earlier, a person who claims to have the right of abode or who holds a current entry clearance is entitled to appeal against any refusal before s/he is removed from the UK. In all other cases the IO should explain that the right of appeal is only exercisable after s/he has left the UK (HC 169 para 91). Before removal, a passenger should be given the opportunity to telephone friends or relatives in this country or his or her Government's representatives in the UK (HC 169 para 87). If a person has a right of appeal before removal, s/he should also be given facilities to communicate with a legal adviser or the UKIAS in order to take advice (HC 169 para 90).

A person who is given leave to enter may, within 12 hours of the conclusion of the examination, be given further notice in writing (see appendix 1 group A) cancelling the earlier decision and refusing leave to enter (Sch 2 para 6(2)). In practice, this nearly always occurs as a result of a subsequent customs check discovering prohibited goods such as drugs in the passenger's baggage.

Where a person is given notice refusing him or her entry to the UK, that notice can at any time be cancelled by notice in writing given by an IO (Sch 2 para 6(3)).

If refused entry, a person can be detained until removed from the UK (Sch 2 paras 8 and 16(2)). However, as an alternative to detention, IOs will very often grant "temporary admission" (Sch 2 para 21(1)). This is the usual practice as regards women, children, and older men, and, indeed, young men are often similary released. (The procedure is used both when it is taking a long time to reach a decision, and after a decision to refuse entry has been taken but before removal.) If temporary admission is not granted, one will have to apply for bail (see chapter 5.2 *(c)*, below) or make representations as to why temporary admission is appropriate on the facts of that case (see chapter 5.2 *(a)* below).

(e) Identifying the stage reached
The law and procedure relating to port refusals have been considered above. Such knowledge should enable one to understand the situation with regard to any individual case.

One may of course be contacted by the would-be entrant, or by his or her relatives and friends, at any time, and it is essential quickly to establish what stage the matter has reached before the appropriate action can be taken. In this respect, both chapter 3.2 above and the questionnaire at appendix 4 provide useful guidelines to follow, and a reminder of which questions should *always* be asked in a port emergency situation.

If it is felt that the particular IO dealing with the case is not being helpful and that certain information required to understand the situation is not forthcoming, one should ask to speak to the CIO. If all else fails one should approach an MP to make enquiries, but normally this will not be necessary.

If the passenger is being detained, it is desirable to visit the place of detention so as to confirm the facts given by the "contact" and by the authorities, and to ensure that the legal position is fully understood by the client.

(f) Categories of port emergencies and procedure to follow
When in full possession of the facts, one will find that the situation falls into one of the categories set out below.

(i) *The passenger has arrived only recently and is currently being interrogated at the port of entry* (See para *(d)*, above.) It may be appropriate to forward information by making representations at this stage (see chapter 5.3 para *(a)* below).

(ii) *The passenger has been either released on temporary admission or is being held in detention pending further enquiries* (See para *(d)*, above.) If in detention, one should attempt to have the passenger released on temporary admission or bail (see chapter 5.2 paras *(a)* and *(c)*). It may be appropriate to forward information by making representations at this stage (see chapter 5.3 para *(a)*).

(iii) *A decision to refuse leave to enter has already been taken* (See paras *(c)* and *(d)*, above.) The person will have been either released on temporary admission or held in detention pending removal.

If the passenger has a right of appeal exercisable from within the UK, the appropriate appeal form should be lodged immediately. Once this has been done, no directions for removal will be given/carried out while the appeal is pending. (The case must then be fully prepared for a hearing before an immigration adjudicator. This falls outside the scope of this book, except to say that such "port refusals" are generally given priority hearing dates and that the representative should not be caught unawares.) An application for temporary admission or bail may be necessary (see chapter 5.2 paras *(a)* and *(c)*, below).

If the passenger has no right of appeal exercisable from within the UK, removal should be prevented by means of a stop order (see chapter 5.1, below) followed by representations (see chapter 5.3) designed to persuade the Minister to reverse the decision. If the passenger is in detention, one should attempt to have him or her released on temporary admission (see chapter 5.2 para *(a)*).

In any event a person refused leave to enter may opt to discontinue his or her fight to have the decision reversed by the appellate authorities or the Minister if it appears that there is little hope of being released from detention in the interim. Voluntary departure, or, rather, allowing oneself to be immediately removed, is always on option at any stage. See the chart on pp24–25.

4.2 Emergencies concerning persons already present in the UK

(a) Assessing the facts

Once initial contact has been made and the facts of the case have emerged, an initial assessment of the problem will be possible. "Identifying the problem" is discussed in outline in chapter 3.3, above, and from that discussion it is clear that the facts will disclose an elementary distinction: either the client will be *seeking* to enter or s/he will have *already* entered. The former category is considered in 4.1, above. Persons who have already entered, but who are now being sought or detained by the immigration authorities, will generally have one of the following problems. Either:

(a) the authorities will be proceeding against them as *deportees*; or
(b) the authorities will be treating them as *illegal entrants*.

Before looking more closely at deportees and illegal entrants, and in order to avoid any confusion, one should note that a passenger seeking entry may also be proceeded against as a deportee or as an illegal entrant. For example, a passenger caught smuggling drugs into the UK will be refused entry and, very often, will eventually be excluded by means of deportation. Further, a passenger seeking to enter the UK in breach of a current deportation order is, by definition (see below), an illegal entrant. This section is not concerned with deportees and illegal entrants as a whole, but simply with persons who as a

Emergencies

(The stages at which they may arise)

PERSONS NOT BEING ALLOWED TO ENTER ON ARRIVAL

PERSONS WHO HAVE *NOT YET* BEEN REFUSED ADMISSION:

Emergency:
- entry may be refused and removal will then be imminent;
- detention pending a decision.

Procedures:
- *fresh application* (any asylum application should be made now if at all possible);
- *representations* that the passenger should be formally or temporarily admitted;
- *temporary admission;*
- *bail;*
- voluntary removal (for the meaning of this term see the box on p.25).

PERSONS WHO HAVE *ALREADY* BEEN REFUSED ADMISSION:

Emergency:
- imminent removal;
- detention pending removal.

Procedures:
- *appeal*, if possible, any decision that leave to enter is required (this will not be possible where prior certificate of entitlement is mandatory);
- *appeal*, if possible, the decision to refuse leave to enter (where, for example, the passenger possesses a valid entry clearance);
- *appeal*, the destination to which passenger is to be removed (generally, can only be brought simultaneously with one of the above two appeals;
- *stop order* followed by
- *representations* (or further representations);
- *judicial review;*
- *temporary admission;*
- *bail* pending an appeal;
- voluntary removal (for the meaning of this term see box below).

PERSONS ALREADY IN THE UK

DEPORTATION ←→ ILLEGAL ENTRY

(see 4.2 para (d))

PERSONS THE SECRETARY OF STATE *MAY DECIDE* TO DEPORT BECAUSE:

1. They have overstayed or broken a condition of their stay (S.3(5)(a)) →

Emergency:
none existing yet, but may try to pre-empt one.

Procedures:

(see 4.2 para (e))

PERSONS THE SECRETARY OF STATE *HAS DECIDED* TO DEPORT UNDER:

1. Section 3(5)(a) →

Emergency:
- deport order may be made;
- now liable to be detained.

Procedures:
- *appeal* the decision (and destination);

(see 4.2 para (f))

PERSONS THE SECRETARY OF STATE *HAS ORDERED* TO BE DEPORTED UNDER:

1. Section 3(5)(a)

Emergency:
- imminent removal in pursuance of order;
- detention pending removal.

Procedures:
- *appeal* the destination if able to;

(see 4.2 para (g))

PERSONS ARRESTED OR ABOUT TO BE ARRESTED, BUT NOT YET TREATED AS ILLEGAL ENTRANTS: →

Emergency:
- if found to be illegal entrants, will face immediate removal;
- detention pending a decision.

Procedures:
- *representations* (oral or written) that

(see 4.2 para (h))

PERSONS TREATED AS ILLEGAL ENTRANTS:

Emergency:
- imminent removal;
- detention pending removal.

Procedures:
- *appeal* against destination;
- *appeal* against validity of removal;

- voluntary removal.

- voluntary removal.

- simply exit the country;
- voluntary removal.

Where the person is not being actively sought, see 4.6.

2. Their deportation would be conducive to the public good (S.3(5)(b))–usually applies to convicted person not recommended by court for deportation

Emergency:
- none existing yet, but may try to pre-empt one.

Procedures:
- *fresh application* (any asylum application *must* be made now if at all possible);
- *representations* against a decision;
- simply exit the country if at liberty.

→ **2.** Section 3(5)(b)

Emergency:
- deport order may be made;
- now liable to be detained/detention may continue once prison sentence completed

Procedures:
- *appeal* the decision (and destination);
- *representations* if appeal fails or none is available;
- *temporary release;*
- *bail* pending an appeal only;
- simply exit the country;
- voluntary removal.

→ **2.** Section 3(5)(b)

Emergency:
- imminent removal in pursuance of order;
- detention pending removal.

Procedures:
- *appeal* the destination if able to;
- *stop order* followed by
- *representations* (or further reps);
- *temporary release;*
- *bail* pending any destination appeal;
- simply exit the country;
- voluntary removal.

3. They are immediate family of a person already ordered to be deported (S.3(5)(c))

Emergency:
none existing yet, but may try to pre-empt one.

Procedures:
- *fresh application* (any asylum application *must* be made now if at all possible);
- *representations* against a decision;
- simply exit the country.

→ **3.** Section 3(5)(c)

Emergency:
- deport order may be made;
- now liable to be detained.

Procedures:
- *appeal* the decision (and destination);
- *representations* if appeal fails or none is available;
- *temporary release;*
- *bail* pending an appeal only;
- simply exit the country;
- *voluntary departure.*

→ **3.** Section 3(5)(c)

Emergency:
- imminent removal in pursuance of order;
- detention pending removal.

Procedures:
- *appeal* the destination if able to;
- *stop order* followed by
- *representations* (or further reps);
- *temporary release;*
- *bail* pending any destination appeal;
- simply exit the country;
- voluntary removal.

4. They are at least 17 and a court, when passing sentence for an imprisonable offence, has recommended deportation (S.3(6))

Emergency:
- deport order may be made as no immigration appeal exists if the recommendation is followed;
- now liable to be detained.

Procedures:
- oppose/appeal the making of a recommendation; and
- when doing so, ask the court to direct release;
- *representations* not to follow the recommendation and requesting
- *temporary release* if the courts fail to direct release;
- *supervised departure;*
- simply exit the country;
- voluntary removal.

(THE MOMENT OF DECISION HAS NO SIGNIFICANCE HERE)

→ **4.** Section 3(6)

Emergency:
- imminent removal in pursuance of order;
- detention pending removal.

Procedures:
- *appeal* the destination;
- *stop order* followed by
- *representations* (or further reps);
- *temporary release;*
- *bail* pending any destination appeal;
- simply exit the country;
- voluntary removal.

WAYS OF LEAVING THE UK

This chart refers to 4 different ways in which a person may leave the UK (apart from involuntarily being removed as an illegal entrant or in pursuance of a deportation order):

1. *"Supervised Departure":* A legally precise term which refers to a formal method by which the immigration authorities may allow certain persons to leave the UK. It is provided for by the Immigration Rules HC 169 paragraph 156 and constitutes an alternative to removal by deportation. Paragraph 156 probably derives from S.5(6) Immigration Act 1971.

2. *"Voluntary Departure":* Again, this is a legally precise term which refers to a formal method by which the immigration authorities may allow certain persons to leave the UK. It is also an alternative to deportation and is provided for by HC168 paragraph 160. Again, it probably derives from S.5(6) of the Act.

3. *"Voluntary Removal":* This is the authors' term and it contemplates persons who agree to be removed as deportees or illegal entrants. Such persons, wishing to leave as soon as possible, will voluntarily waive, withdraw or discontinue any appeal, representation or other procedure. Accordingly, depending on the stage that has been reached, voluntary removal may be instantaneous or may have to be expedited.

4. *"Simply Exiting the Country":* Again, this is a term of the authors' and it refers to persons who are at liberty, who possess their passports, and who simply embark without the knowledge of or any arrangement with, the immigration authorities. A deportation order made in respect of any such person will only be revoked if s/he exited before the order was made.

matter of fact have already passed through a port of entry and are now in the UK.

(b) Is the client being proceeded against as a deportee or an illegal entrant?
The law concerning who may or may not be deported, and who is or is not an illegal entrant, is at best complex and at worst uncertain. Happily, though, this need not concern the person who is simply dealing with the emergency. The purpose of emergency proceedings is not to challenge appropriateness or validity, but rather to prevent a client's imminent removal from the UK and, if detained, to secure his or her release. The substantive challenge (if any) will come later, once the immediate emergency has been contained and expert advice enlisted.

The easiest way to determine whether the client is being proceeded against by way of deportation or an allegation of illegal entry is to identify the formal notices which have been issued to the client by the immigration authorities. The notices in common use are reproduced in appendix 1 groups C and D. If no useful documentation is available, one will simply have to enquire when initial contact with the appropriate authority is made (see appendix 2 and, further, below).

(c) Identifying the stage the authorities have reached in dealing with the client
It is essential to appreciate that the precise nature of a deportation or illegal entry emergency (and, therefore, the way in which to deal with it) may vary depending on the stage that has been reached.

DEPORTATION

(a) the Secretary of State is *able* to decide to make a deportation order, but the *decision* has not yet been made; or
(b) the Secretary of State has *decided* to make a deportation order, but the *order* has not yet been made; or
(c) the Secretary of State has made a deportation order but the deportee has not yet been removed.

ILLEGAL ENTRY

(a) an arrest has been or will be made but formal notice treating the recipient as an illegal entrant has not yet been served; or
(b) formal notice has been served but the alleged illegal entrant has not yet been removed.

These stages, together with the basic law that is involved, will now be considered individually. The emergency procedures that may be applied at each stage will also be indicated. See also the chart on pp24–25, which summarises the following paragraphs.

(d) Before any decision to deport
British citizens cannot be deported (ss3(5) and 6(2)). "British citizen" includes

any person who has the right of abode in the UK (s2(2), as amended by the British Nationality Act 1981 s39(2)). Further, a deportation order generally cannot be made against a Commonwealth citizen or citizen of the Republic of Ireland who has been ordinarily resident in the UK ever since the 1971 Act came into force on 1 January 1973 (s7). All other persons are liable to deportation in certain circumstances (see below and p34).

If one is consulted by a person who is liable to deportation but in respect of whom a decision to deport has not yet been made, then there are times when one might try to pre-empt such a decision by making representations or a fresh application (for example where a visitor has overstayed and now wants to study, one may make application for leave to remain as a student and advance an apology and excuse in respect of the overstay). Although one should act without delay in such situations, an actual "emergency" will not yet exist. Accordingly, such cases are considered in 4.6.

However, there is one particular situation which is better dealt with here: where a person who is at least 17 years of age is convicted of an offence punishable with imprisonment, when sentencing that person the court may recommend that s/he be deported (ss3(6) and 6).

Where the Secretary of State acts in pursuance of such a recommendation, he cannot be appealed within the immigration system (see HC 169 para 150). Accordingly, there is no need for the Secretary of State to give formal notice of his intention to deport someone in pursuance of a court recommendation (under the Notice Regulations 1984 reg 3(1) only an *appealable* decision must be notified). In such cases, therefore, there is little to distinguish the making of a decision to deport from the making of the deportation order itself. If procedures associated with emergencies are not applied, the recommendation will normally be followed by a deportation order and removal.

As stated, a court, when passing sentence on a person who is liable to deportation and who has been convicted of an imprisonable offence, may recommend that person for deportation.

(i) *Urgency* The situation will not usually be urgent in that the Secretary of State will not act while an appeal may be brought against the recommendation. Although a recommendation (and a deportation decision made in pursuance of one) cannot be challenged within the immigration appeals system, it may be appealed within the courts in the same way as any other sentence. A recommendation made by magistrates may be appealed to the Crown Court within 21 days, and one made by the Crown Court may be appealed to the Court of Appeal within 28 days.

Further, if the sentence also includes a term of immediate imprisonment, the Secretary of State will be unlikely to consider the question of deportation until several weeks prior to completion of the prison sentence.

(ii) *Detention and release* Unless the court, when recommending deportation, specifically directs release (once any prison sentence has been served), the convicted person will be detained (Sch 3 para 2(1)). In such instances, though, the Secretary of State may nevertheless direct release pending further consideration of the case (Sch 3 para 2(1)) or, if the recommendation is appealed, the court considering the appeal may direct release even if that appeal fails (Sch 3 para 2(1A)).

(iii) *Advised procedures* The sentencing court should be urged (in the course of mitigation in open court) not to make a recommendation (see *R v Nazari* [1980] 3 All ER 880, CA for guidelines). The court should be asked to direct release if it is minded to make a recommendation (see chapter 5.2 para *(b)*). Where a recommendation is made, serious consideration should be given to the question of an appeal. A surprising number of recommendations by magistrates are very obviously appealable. If necessary, the court considering any appeal should be requested at an oral hearing to direct release and/or a request for temporary release should be put to the Secretary of State (see chapter 5.2 para *(b)* for details).

Where no criminal appeal against the recommendation is brought, or where the appeal is dismissed, one should then make *representations* to the Secretary of State urging him not to make a deportation order (for representations generally, see chapter 5.3).

If the client wishes to leave the UK as soon as possible rather than attempt to stay, *supervised departure* may be arranged (see chapter 5.7 para *(b)*).

(e) Once a decision to deport has been made

Apart from deportation in pursuance of a court recommendation (s3(6)), the Secretary of State can decide to make a deportation order under s3(5), which covers three different situations.

(i) *Overstayers and persons who have failed to observe a condition (s3(5)(a))* The majority of s3(5) decisions involve overstayers. These, quite simply, are persons who after entering the UK have failed to apply for leave to remain or whose applications have been refused (see appendix 1 group B).

(ii) *Persons whose deportation is conducive to the public good (s3(5)(b))* Most s3(5)(b) decisions are taken in respect of persons who have been convicted of an offence but who have not been recommended for deportation by the sentencing court.

(iii) *Immediate family of a person whose deportation has already been ordered (s3(5)(c))* The "immediate family" of a deportee means a man's wife and their children under 18, or a woman's children under 18 (s5(4)). Section 3(5)(c) decisions are the least common and cannot be made more than eight weeks after the deportee has left the UK (s5(3)).

(iv) *Urgency* A person against whom a s3(5) decision has been taken is not in any immediate danger of being removed in that a general right of appeal exists (s15(1)(a)) and no order can be made until the time in which to appeal has passed or until the appeal has failed (s15(2)). However, an emergency may exist in connection with the giving of notice of appeal.

(v) *Arrest and detention* As there is a general right of appeal against a decision taken under s3(5), the Secretary of State is under a duty to give formal notice of any such decision (Notice Regulations 1984 reg 3(1)); see appendix 1 group C. Once this notice has been given, the person concerned is liable to be detained (Sch 3 para 2(2)). However, the Secretary of State may decide (or may be persuaded) not to use this power (see Sch 3 paras 5 and 6(b)). Further, once notice of appeal has been given bail may be available (Sch 3 para 3; Sch 2 para 29(1)).

Once a person is liable to be detained by virtue of being served with notice of a deportation decision, s/he may be arrested without warrant by a constable or an IO, and a constable may obtain a warrant to enter premises, by force if necessary, in order to search for and arrest such a person (Sch 3 para 2(4); Sch 2 para 17). Further, once detained, an IO, constable or prison officer may take all reasonable steps to photograph and identify the detainee and to ascertain his or her nationality (Sch 3 para 2(4); Sch 2 para 18(2) and (3)).

(vi) *Advised procedures* Unless in receipt of expert advice to the contrary, one should always appeal against the decision to deport (see the chart on pp38–39 below for time limits and chapter 5.5 para *(c)* for how to give notice of appeal, whether in time or out of time). If the client is in detention, one should try to obtain temporary release or bail (see chapter 5.2 paras *(b)* and *(c)*). However, if the decision was taken under s3(5)(b), the client may well be serving a prison sentence, in which case immediate release will of course be impossible. If the client wishes to leave the UK, voluntary departure may be arranged (see chapter 5.7 para *(a)*). Finally, representations may be appropriate (for example, representations against the making of an order where any appeal has been unsuccessful or where leave to appeal out of time has not been given). For representations generally, see chapter 5.3, below.

(f) Once a deportation order has been made

Once the time limit in which to appeal a s3(5) decision has passed (or once the appeal has ultimately been withdrawn or dismissed), a deportation order may be prepared and submitted to the Secretary of State for his signature (for an example, see appendix 1 group C). A s3(6) decision, on the other hand, can be taken only once the criminal courts have finished with any appeal against the deportation recommendation; once taken, *no* immigration appeal exists against that decision and so the deportation order itself can be prepared immediately and submitted to the Secretary of State for his signature.

As a matter of practice, before the Secretary of State signs any deportation order he will consider the facts of the case as well as "any other relevant information, whether or not it was available to the courts or the appellate authorities" (HC 169 para 167). It is for this reason that it is advisable to make representations (above). If any such representations are unsuccessful, the order will be signed and served on the deportee.

(i) *Urgency* When a deportation order is in force against any person, the Secretary of State may give directions for that person's removal to a specific destination (Sch 3 para 1(1)). However, the deportee's actual removal from the UK will not necessarily be imminent because s/he may still have a right of appeal against the destination specified in the "removal directions" (s17(1)(b)). The 1971 Act complicates destination appeals by requiring them to be brought, if at all possible, in the context of any appeal against the actual decision to make a deportation order (see the appeals and time limits chart on pp38–39; and see chapter 5.5). Suffice it here to say that launching a destination appeal, irrespective of its merits, is a very useful way in which to buy time. Once a destination appeal is brought, all removal directions will cease to have effect while the appeal is pending (Sch 3 para 3; Sch 2 para 28(2)).

(ii) *Arrest and detention* If the deportee is not already in detention (see para *(e)*(v) above) s/he may be detained under the authority of the Secretary of State pending removal (Sch 3 para 2(3)). However, the Secretary of State may decide (or may be persuaded) not to use this power. The law regarding bail pending appeal used to be thought of as unsatisfactory in that it seemed bail could not be obtained without the consent of the Secretary of State (Sch 3 para 3; Sch 2 para 30(1)). It has now been held that his consent to bail is *not* required (see *Alghali* [1984] Imm AR 106, QBD).

A person who is liable to be detained may be arrested without a warrant by a constable or an IO (Sch 3 para 2(4); Sch 2 para 17(1)) and a constable may obtain a warrant to enter premises, by force if necessary, in order to search for and arrest such a person (Sch 3 para 2(4); Sch 2 para 17(2)). Further, a constable, IO or prison officer may take any reasonable steps to photograph or otherwise identify a detainee or to determine his or her nationality (Sch 3 para 2(4); Sch 2 para 18(2) and (3)). See also chapter 5.2 para *(b)* below.

To launch an appeal against destination will not affect a person's liability to be arrested and detained (Sch 3 para 3; Sch 2 para 18(3)).

(iii) *Advised procedures* In order to buy time in which to obtain expert assistance, removal should be prevented by bringing a destination appeal if this is possible (see the chart on pp38–39 and chapter 5.5 para *(c)*). Alternatively, one may use a stop order to prevent removal pending the consideration of representations (see chapter 5.1 and 5.3 respectively). If the client is in detention, one should try to obtain temporary release (see chapter 5.2 para *(b)*) or bail (chapter 5.2 para *(c)*).

(iv) *Removal* If all efforts fail, the Deportation Machinery Group at the Home Office will proceed to remove the deportee. If necessary, the police will see to details such as ensuring that the deportee's passport is valid (see Sch 3 para 2(4); Sch 2 para 18(3)). If it is necessary to contact the police in order to assist a detained deportee, the Aliens Registration section of the local police station should be telephoned, or in London, the Deportation Section of the Aliens Registration Office (see appendix 2). Further, a visit to a detained deportee may be arranged but express permission will be required before personal belongings may be passed over in the course of a visit.

The police will then take the detained deportee to the appropriate port. Under the authority of an IO, s/he can then be placed on board the ship or aircraft and the captain can be required to prevent the passenger from disembarking until the removal directions have been fulfilled (Sch 3 para 1(3); Sch 2 paras 11 and 16(4)—see the IS83A at appendix 1 group G). In order to do so, the captain could detain the passenger in custody on board, though usually he will simply retain the passenger's passport. Finally, any money belonging to the deportee may be used by the Secretary of State to cover the costs of deportation (Sch 3 para 4), but the passenger should never be left without a little cash for the journey.

(g) Persons arrested or about to be arrested for suspected illegal entry
An illegal entrant is a person "unlawfully entering or seeking to enter in breach of a deportation order or of the immigration laws, and includes also a person who has so entered" (s33(1)). This definition includes not only persons who have entered the UK by clandestinely avoiding immigration control but also those who have gained entry by fraud or deception when passing *through* immigration control (*Khawaja and Khera* [1983] 1 All ER 765). However, persons who are in breach of a condition of their leave are *not* necessarily illegal entrants. For example, a visitor who works despite a prohibition on employment is not necessarily someone who has gained entry by deceiving an IO. Further, it is now accepted that a Commonwealth citizen who entered before 9 March 1968 cannot be an illegal entrant even if s/he has subsequently re-entered in the same false identity (Home Office letter to MP, 18 January 1981).

(i) *Urgency* Until satisfied that the suspect is indeed an illegal entrant, directions for the removal of that person will not be given. This stage may be reached almost immediately, or it may take a day or two. As a matter of practice, a form called an IS 151A will be served once it is thought that the suspect *is* an illegal entrant and therefore liable to removal (see appendix 1 group D). On the basis that it is always easier to prevent a decision from being made rather than to have it reversed, every effort should be made to prevent an IO from deciding that it would be appropriate to serve an IS 151A.

(ii) *Arrest and detention* A suspected illegal entrant may come to be arrested (and held) on varying bases. Under the 1971 Act there is a power to detain (and, therefore, an implicit power to arrest) a person "who may be required to submit to examination" as well as a person "in respect of whom (removal) directions may be given" (Sch 2 para 16(1) and (2)). Further, the

Act also makes illegal entry an offence (s24(1)(a)), though charges are very rarely brought. Nevertheless, a constable or an IO may arrest without warrant anyone who with "reasonable cause" is suspected of being an illegal entrant (s24(2)). Alternatively, the question of illegal entry may first be raised as a result of police enquiries made in respect of a person "helping the police" with a wholly different matter.

These legal bases upon which a person may be questioned involve different remedies when it comes to securing that person's release. For present purposes suffice it to say that if the authorities are seriously considering proceeding on the basis of illegal entry then, usually, they will either serve an IS 151A or simply state that the person is being detained under the Immigration Act (ie Sch 2 para 16), in which case the remedy is "temporary release".

(iii) *Advised procedures* Where the authorities have *not* yet decided that they ought to proceed on the basis of illegal entry, one should try to determine what, exactly, is the nature of the suspicion. One should then try to counter that suspicion by, for example, gathering evidence and/or making written or oral representations (see chapter 5.3). The time may come when habeas corpus proceedings may be appropriate (see chapter 5.6 para *(a)*) but, in the meanwhile, if the alleged illegal entrant is being held under Sch 2, temporary release should be requested under Sch 2 para 21(1) (see chapter 5.2 para *(b)*). Where the suspected person has not yet been arrested or detained, voluntary departure may well be preferable (see chapter 5.7 para *(a)*).

(h) Persons considered to be illegal entrants

If, having considered all aspects of the case, the IO is satisfied that the suspect is an illegal entrant, form IS 151A will be served (see appendix 1 group D). Removal directions may then be made (Sch 2 para 9) and detention may commence or continue (Sch 2 para 16(2)).

As has already been explained, prospective deportees, apart from a destination appeal, will generally also have a substantive right of appeal (an appeal against sentence for those whose sentence includes a deportation recommendation and, for others, an immigration appeal against a decision to deport). Persons considered to be illegal entrants, however, are in a much worse position. *Some* illegal entrants (those whose entry was illegal because a current deportation order was in force against them at the time) may appeal no more than destination before being removed (s17(1)(c)), and a rare few (those whose entry was in breach of a deportation order but who claim not to be the person named in that order) may appeal no more than the legal correctness of the removal directions before having to leave (s16(1)(a)). For this reason, practitioners have increasingly relied on a long-standing jurisdiction of the High Court which allows the Queen's Bench Division of that court to review administrative actions. This is known as a judicial review. Also available from the Queen's Bench Division (and also used by practitioners) is a device known as a writ of habeas corpus. Judicial review and habeas corpus are briefly compared and discussed in chapter 5.6, below.

(i) *Urgency* From the above it will be clear that the great majority of persons treated as illegal entrants are in a position similar to the great majority of passengers refused entry into the UK (see 4.1, above). That is to say, they have no right of appeal exercisable from within the UK and they face imminent removal with the prospect of detention until that time. Once the IS 151A has been served, removal directions will be given at the same time or will follow shortly. Immediate action to prevent removal will almost invariably be required.

(ii) *Arrest and detention* Being liable to removal (Sch 2 para 9), a person treated as an illegal entrant "may be detained under the authority of an immigration officer pending the giving of directions and pending . . . removal" (Sch 2 para 16(2)). A person detained in this way may nevertheless be granted temporary release, but this will not prejudice a later exercise of the power to detain (Sch 2 para 21(1)). Further, bail may be available if an immigration appeal is pending (Sch 2 para 29(1)) and it is immaterial whether or not the Secretary of State in accordance with Sch 2 para 30(1) consents to bail (see *Aghali* [1984] Imm AR 106, QBD).

(iii) *Advised procedures* One should obtain a stop order so that representations may be made to the effect that the person is not an illegal entrant or that his or her stay should in any event be regularised (see chapter 5.1 and 5.3 respectively). It may be possible to appeal the destination specified in removal directions, or the validity of those directions (see the chart on pp38–39 and chapter 5.5 para *(c)*). Further, habeas corpus proceedings may be possible or one may move for judicial review of the decision to treat the person as an illegal entrant, or of the Secretary of State's response to the representations (see chapter 5.6, below). Temporary release should be requested if the person is detained (see chapter 5.2 para *(b)*). If possible, one should apply for bail (see chapter 5.2 para *(c)*). On the other hand, if the person simply wishes to be removed from the UK as soon as possible, voluntary departure may be arranged (see chapter 5.7 para *(a)*).

(iv) *Removal* The procedure has been dealt with in para *(f)*(iv).

4.3 Immigration offences

The wide variety of statutory offences include a selection from the Immigration Act 1971 Pt III (see appendix 6). These offences concern illegal entry, staying beyond a time limit, breach of a condition, assisting illegal entry, harbouring and various other immigration-related matters. Facilitating illegal entry (s25(1)) is the only indictable offence, the others being "summary only".

Immigration offences should generally be viewed in the same way as other criminal offences when it comes to emergencies concerning arrest, bail and the like. In respect of the more serious immigration offences a constable *or* an IO may arrest without warrant anyone who has or who is reasonably suspected to have committed or attempted to commit such an offence (see ss24(2) and 25(3)). Once arrested, suspects will usually be questioned at the local police station. If charged and remanded in custody, they will be transferred to a remand wing of a prison in the normal way.

Administrative proceedings against persons who may be deported under s3(5)(c) for staying beyond a time limit and against persons who may be illegal entrants have been discussed above. Additionally, overstaying and illegal entry are both immigration offences (s24(1)(b)(i) and (1)(a) respectively), so *criminal* proceedings will also be possible (see s28(4)). However, neither police nor immigration officers are particularly interested in prosecuting illegal entrants, who may in any event swiftly be removed from the UK. The position with regard to overstayers is somewhat different: if the immigration authorities only are involved, criminal charges will be rare. However, if the overstayer is arrested or questioned by the police in relation to some other matter, then charges under s24(1)(b)(i) will frequently be brought if enquiries reveal the suspect's true immigration status. Presumably, the police interest in proceeding with such prosecutions (but not illegal entry cases) is to obtain a deportation recommendation from the sentencing court and thereby ensure the defendant's likely removal from the UK.

A deportation recommendation may be made by any court having the power to sentence the defendant (s6(1)) and it may be challenged only by way of an appeal against sentence (see 4.2 para *(d)*, above). A person against whom a deportation recommendation exists should be considered in the context of 4.2, above. Similarly, defendants who are subject to immigration control but against whom *no* recommendation has been made may also need to be considered in the context of 4.2 in that there will still be a risk of deportation under s3(5)(b) (deportation conducive to the public good).

Finally, where it is clear that a person serving a prison sentence will be leaving the UK upon release (whether by formal removal or otherwise—see chapter 5.7), then the local review committee should be advised as it may be in favour of an early release on parole.

4.4 Time limits

(a) The problem

When practitioners talk about emergencies, they tend only to refer to the areas covered in 4.1 and 4.2, above (ie the detention and removal of passengers arriving and persons already here). However, the need to act prior to the approaching expiry of a time limit can, and often does, constitute as much of an emergency. Although no "time limit" emergency involves securing a client's release from detention, most do concern the prevention of imminent or eventual removal from the UK, or the prevention of certain exclusion from entering or re-entering. Generally, time limit emergencies are much more easily dealt with than the emergencies already discussed, and will usually involve no more than the posting of an application or notice, the sending of a telex, or the simple giving of advice. Nevertheless, these steps will in all cases be critical to the client's welfare and in all cases should be viewed as the handling of an emergency.

The principal time limit emergencies are as follows:

Immigration

(a) returning residents and originating applications for children under 18;
(b) applications for extensions or variation;
(c) appeals.

Nationality Remaining within the residential requirements for registration/naturalisation.

Criminal Appealing against deportation recommendations.

(b) Immigration

(i) *Returning residents and children under 18 years old* Persons whose passports are endorsed with indefinite leave to enter or remain in the UK may stay here as long as they wish and will not be subject to employment restrictions or any other condition (see s3(3)(a)). Nevertheless, such persons are still subject to immigration control (unlike those who have the "right of abode"—see chapter 2.2, above). The Immigration Rules therefore can and do regulate their movement: a person with indefinite leave who has been absent for *up to two years* is *entitled* to re-enter (HC 169 para 56); but one who has been absent for *longer than two years* can only re-enter at the *discretion* of the immigration authorities (HC 169 para 57). There are various situations in which an absence in excess of two years will not matter a great deal (see appendix 3 for further reading) but suffice it for present purposes to say that a person with indefinite leave should generally be sure to re-enter the UK within two years of any departure.

When consulted by or on behalf of a returning resident, the "two-year" rule should be carefully explained. Immediate return to the UK may be necessary. An alternative procedure arises from the fact that anyone intending to travel to the UK may first establish his or her eligibility to do so by applying to the nearest British post for an "entry clearance" (HC 169 paras 10, 11). On a strict interpretation HC 169 para 56 requires physical re-entry within two years, but in practice it will suffice if the entrant possesses a current entry clearance *applied for* prior to the expiry of the two-year period. Accordingly, as an alternative to immediate return, one may simply apply for a returning resident's entry clearance. Mostly, an entry clearance application must either be made by the applicant in person or bear his or her signature. Practice varies, though, so it is better to cover all avenues: if time is short, then in addition to advising the returning resident to apply, one should also apply on his or her behalf. If it turns out that only the representative's application was made in time, the entry clearance officer will often treat the properly-made application as having been made on that earlier date.

Parents settled or settling in the UK may be joined or accompanied by their unmarried children under 18 years old (HC 169 para 50). Assuming that they are subject to immigration control (see chapter 2.2, above), such children *must* obtain entry clearance before travelling to the UK (HC 169 para 47). Once a child turns 18, it will be practically impossible to come and settle in the UK (see HC 169 para 51). As far as age is concerned, the critical moment is *not* the date of physical entry, but the date of application for entry clearance (HC 169 paras 13(b) and 173). As with returning residents, an application signed only by a representative will often not suffice. This problem will arise only rarely, though, in that almost invariably at least one parent will be available in the UK to sign the application.

In cases involving returning residents and children under 18, one should always bear in mind the possible time limit emergency. The deadline will usually still be far off, but there are times when an emergency application will be required (see chapter 5.5 for the making of applications).

(ii) *Applications for extensions and variation* Persons whose passports are endorsed with limited leave to enter or remain may apply to the Secretary of State for that leave to be extended or varied (s3(3)(a)). If an application is made *after* the limited leave has expired, then, although the application will be considered, there will be no right of appeal against any refusal. Further, from the moment leave expires the person will be an overstayer. On the other hand, if the application is made *before* leave expires the applicant will automatically be given an extension until 28 days after the Secretary of State's decision (Immigration (Variation of Leave) Order 1976 SI No 1572 art 3(1)). Further, a right of appeal will then exist against any refusal of the application and the appellant will not be required to leave the UK pending the final outcome of that appeal (s14(1)). A case in which the client's limited leave is about to expire should be viewed as an emergency.

If an emergency situation exists, the client or his or her representative should immediately make at least a "holding" application (see chapter 5.5 for the making of applications).

(iii) *Appeals* The immigration appeals system consists of a two-tier structure: adjudicators (at various hearing centres around the UK) and the Tribunal (in London only). In respect of every appealable decision made or action taken by the immigration authorities there is a *right* of appeal to an adjudicator (ss13–17). If the appeal is dismissed by the adjudicator, one may then appeal to the Tribunal but *leave* to do so must be applied for and granted (Immigration Appeals (Procedure) Rules 1984 SI No 2041 r 14(1)). Some appeals against a decision to make a deportation order lie direct to the Tribunal at first instance (s15(7)–(9)).

In order to bring an adjudicator appeal, one must *give notice of appeal* (see

Procedure Rules 1984 r6) to the immigration authority which took the decision (see rr6(2) and 44(1)(c) and (d)). In order to bring a Tribunal appeal, one must *apply for leave to appeal* (r16) and direct that application to either the adjudicator (r15(1)) or to the Tribunal (r15(2)) for consideration. However, all notices of appeal and applications for leave to appeal are subject to time limits (rr4 and 15, respectively). When notice of appeal to an adjudicator is given out of time, there is a *discretion* to accept it nevertheless, if by virtue of special circumstances it would be just and right to do so (r5). However, there is *no discretion* to accept a late application for leave to appeal (*Armstrong* [1977] Imm AR 84).

As far as the giving of a notice of appeal is concerned, the time limits are set out in the chart on pp38–39. In relation to applications for leave to appeal, an application directed to an adjudicator must be made "forthwith" once that adjudicator has dismissed the first instance appeal (r15(1)). For present purposes, one should not choose to direct an application to the adjudicator, so no more need be said of that alternative. An application for leave to appeal which is directed to the *Tribunal* must be made within 14 days of the dismissal of the appeal by the adjudicator (if the appellant is in the Common Travel Area (CTA)) or within 42 days (if s/he is outside the CTA (r15(3))). The CTA comprises the UK, Channel Islands, Isle of Man and the Irish Republic (see HC 169 para 8).

It is of course self-evident that where a time limit is about to end, immediate action will be required. How to give notice of appeal or apply for leave (both generally and as a matter of urgency) is discussed in chapter 5.5.

(c) Nationality

Certain provisions of the British Nationality Act 1981 require applicants for naturalisation and *some* applicants for registration to fulfil a residential requirement; that is to say, they must live in the UK for a specified length of time before becoming eligible to apply for British citizenship. The Act also specifies the maximum permitted absences. Determining whether or not the residential requirements have been met (or the nearest date on which they will be met) is simply a matter of arithmetic. Persons who go abroad frequently or for long periods are often very distressed to learn that although they *could* have applied for citizenship in the recent past, that opportunity has been lost as a result of the pattern and duration of their absences. Such persons will usually find themselves having *again to begin* a three-year or five-year qualifying period.

The two important formulae are as follows:

(a) five-year qualifying period—maximum permitted absence of 450 days with no more than 90 of those days falling within the final 12 months. This applies principally to:
   (i)) aliens and Commonwealth citizens naturalising in their own right (British Nationality Act 1981 Sch 1 para 1(2));
   (ii) British Dependent Territories citizens, British Overseas citizens,

IMMIGRATION APPEALS AND TIME LIMITS

It is not essential to memorise the various time limits in that when an immigration authority gives formal notice of an appealable decision, that notice will explain how to bring an appeal and the applicable time limit will be clearly stated (see appendix 1 group G). Nevertheless, the chart below may serve as a useful reminder of the principal appeal rights and their time limit.

Principal situations in which an appeal exists	Time limit
PERSONS OUTSIDE THE UK may almost always appeal (S.13(2) against refusal by the British post abroad to issue an "entry clearance" (prior proof of one's eligibility to enter under the Immigration Rules) or a "certificate of entitlement" (proof that one is not subject to immigration control).	3 months (Rule 4(2), (4)).
PASSENGERS ARRIVING AT SEA/AIRPORT (a) may *sometimes* appeal against a decision that "leave" is required (ie, a decision that the passenger is subject to immigration control) S.13(1)—see 2.2, above). One can choose to appeal from within or outside the UK. →	*Before* removal or up to 28 days *after* removal (Rule 4(1)(b)).
OR (b) passengers who *are* subject to control (i) may *sometimes* appeal from *within* the UK against refusal of "leave of enter" (S.13(1)—see 4.1); →	*before removal or up to 28 days after* removal (Rule 4(1)(b)).
(ii) may *almost always* appeal from *outside* the UK against such a refusal (S.13(1)). →	can only appeal *after* departure from UK, but not later than 28 days after (Rule 4(1)(a)).
AND (c) *if* under (a) or (b) above, there is a right of appeal which may be exercised *within* the UK, then in exercising that right the passenger may at the same time appeal the *destination* to which s/he may be removed (see S.17(5); S.13(3)) →	NOT APPLICABLE (as the destination appeal will be simultaneous with main appeal).

proceedings are under way (S.14(1)).	(Rule 4(5)).
PROSPECTIVE DEPORTEES (a) except for proceedings in pursuance of a court recommendation, a deportation *decision* (i.e. the *intention* to make a deportation *order*) can almost always be appealed (S.15(1)(a)—see 4.2 para (e)). The appellant cannot be removed while appeal proceedings are under way (S.15(2)) and, except for "overstayers" the appeal will usually be direct to the Tribunal at first instance (see S.15(7)–(9)). →	14 days (Rule 4(7)).
AND (b) *whether or not* there is a right of appeal under (a) above, all prospective deportees will generally be able to appeal against the destination to which they may be removed (S.17(1)(b)). However, where an appeal under (a) above exists and is brought, then if the destination has been formally notified it will have to be appealed at the same time (S.17(4)). →	NOT APPLICABLE (as the destination appeal will be simultaneous with the main appeal).
NB: if the destination is *not* officially notified in time, or if no appeal against the deportation decision exists or is brought, then the prospective deportee will be able to bring a *separate* appeal against the destination (S.17(1)(b)). →	14 days from the giving of removal directions (Rule 4(10)(b)).
ALLEGED ILLEGAL ENTRANTS (a) a person considered to be an illegal entrant has no right of appeal against the *decision* that s/he is an illegal entrant, but may appeal against the *validity* of the directions given for his/her removal from the UK (ie the *merits* of the case are irrelevant—only the *legal correctness* of the removal directions may be challenged (S.16(1)(a)—see 4.2 para (h)). This very limited form of appeal (i) may *extremely rarely* be brought from within the UK (S.16(2)), in which case one may choose to appeal from within or outside the UK; →	*before* removal from the UK or up to 28 days *after* removal (Rule 4(9)(b)).
(ii) will *almost always* be exercisable only from *outside* the UK. →	can only appeal *after* departure from the UK, but not later than 28 days after (Rule 4(9)(a)).
AND (b) *whether or not* there is a right of appeal under (a)(i), above, an alleged illegal entrant will be able to appeal against the destination to which s/he may be removed *but only if the basis of the illegal entry is that s/he entered the UK in defiance of a current deportation order* (S.17(1)(c)). →	14 days from the giving of removal directions (Rule 4(10)(b)).
THE ABOVE APPEAL RIGHTS COME FROM SECTIONS 13–17 OF THE IMMIGRATION ACT 1971.	THE ABOVE TIME LIMITS COME FROM RULE 4 OF THE PROCEDURE RULES 1984.

British subjects and British Protected Persons registering by entitlement (s4(1)–(4));

(b) three-year qualifying period—maximum permitted absence of 270 days with no more than 90 of those days falling within the final 12 months. This applies principally to naturalisation by the spouse of a British citizen (Sch 1 para 3(a)–(d)).

Both the five-year and three-year qualifying periods must start and end on days when the applicant was physically present in the UK.

Persons falling into any of the above categories who intend to apply for British citizenship should be advised of the appropriate formula. The general rule of thumb is that any person who *might possibly* spend up to a quarter of his or her time outside the UK should take extreme care. This is especially important in respect of persons with indefinite leave to remain in the UK who plan their absences solely according to the rule that to qualify as a returning resident one need only touch UK soil once every two years (HC 169 para 56, see p35, above). For further reading on nationality, see appendix 3.

(d) Criminal

Where a deportation recommendation has been made by a court passing sentence, the time limit for appealing from a magistrates' court to the Crown Court is 21 days, and from the Crown Court to the Court of Appeal 28 days.

4.5 Financial distress

A person may require urgent legal advice in connection with the fact that s/he is in financial crisis. Normally one's thoughts should be directed to whether that person is eligible for any of a number of benefits or services provided by the welfare state. However, eligibility for welfare benefits can be dependent upon one's immigration status. Further, even if a person can theoretically claim a particular benefit, it must be considered whether it is in his or her longer-term interests to do so in view of the adverse immigration consequences (for example, refusal of extensions) which may result.

The Immigration Rules stipulate that many categories of persons admitted to the UK have to maintain and accommodate themselves "without recourse to public funds". Paragraph 1 of HC 169 as amended by HC 503 defines "public funds" as supplementary benefit, family income supplement and housing under the Housing (Homeless Persons) Act 1977 (as consolidated in the Housing Act 1985 Pt III, which comes into force on 1 April 1986). It should be noted that this definition *excludes* many other social security benefits such as unemployment benefit, sickness/invalidity and disablement benefit, widow's benefit, retirement pensions, child and one-parent benefit. Student grants also fall outside the scope of "public funds".

Whether the Home Office will decide to take a negative view of the claiming of benefits and services will depend on both the *precise immigration status* of the person claiming and the *exact benefit* that is being claimed. This is a huge and intricate topic and one which cannot be discussed within the limitations of this book. Rather, this brief mention of "financial emergencies" in an immigration context is intended as a warning of the potential dangers.

Even if the client is apparently concerned solely with his or her financial predicament, this may be only because of lack of knowledge about the wider issues, rather than due to a basic lack of concern. It may be that s/he would prefer hardship (particularly if it involved something less than total destitution, and was thought likely to be of limited rather than permanent duration) rather than to jeopardise his or her future stay in the UK. Whatever financial emergency exists, if there is any doubt in the adviser's mind as to the possible immigration consequences of a particular claim, this should be fully investigated *before* the claim is made. If it emerges that there is indeed some risk involved, the matter must be explained to the client and his or her instructions taken.

It should be noted both that there are a number of specialist organisations who give advice on this area of law, and that a specialist text on the subject has been published (see appendices 2 and 3 respectively).

4.6 Avoiding emergencies

So far, the various emergency situations that can arise have been described. Obviously, it is desirable if such potential emergencies can be either foreseen or altogether prevented.

For example, if informed that a passenger is due shortly to arrive at a port of entry, one should obtain some details in advance and give the person meeting the passenger a telephone number through which an adviser can be contacted if problems arise. Indeed, sometimes it will be necessary to advise a person to come to the UK even when one knows that on arrival s/he will be interviewed at length and, very probably, initially be given only temporary admission. In such cases one should arrange with the passenger (and sponsor) precisely when s/he should arrive. This procedure is particularly appropriate where the intended passenger claims British citizenship by descent (see chapter 2.2, above).

In other immigration situations the clients often create the emergency from which they must then be extricated. However, legal advisers with little experience in the field can cause great harm through making ill-judged and often totally hopeless applications. An extremely large number of those persons who have been removed from the UK as deportees and illegal entrants were "discovered" by the authorities as a result of their own approaches to the Home Office.

In particular, it should be appreciated that, in making an application to "regularise" an unlawful stay, there is often an element of risk involved. (The degree of risk depends upon the facts of the individual case.) It may well be that the client is prepared to take the risk, but s/he should nevertheless be informed of its existence.

Where there is no shadow of a doubt that contacting the Home Office on behalf of an illegal entrant or deportee whose existence and whereabouts are not known to the authorities will result in instant removal, the client would be better advised simply to exit the country. Alternatively, the client may choose simply to continue as before until such time as there is another amnesty or until his or her circumstances change so as to make regularisation by the Home Office more likely.

Apart from avoiding emergencies by *refraining* from contacting the Home Office, many immigration emergencies could simply and surely be avoided by an *early approach.* An early approach will be possible only where a person seeks advice at an early stage, but all too often the adviser does not think to act immediately.

EXAMPLE

M was a student who applied for an extension 10 days after his previous leave expired. Accordingly, he had no right of appeal when the Home Office refused his application. He sought advice at once and, correctly, was told to collect evidence to rebut the reasons for refusal. That evidence would be sent to the Home Office together with representations. However, the adviser failed to make initial (or "holding") representations. Two months later M was arrested and charged with overstaying and a deportation recommendation was made.

Had holding representations been made, the Home Office would not have passed the case to the police and M would not now be a convicted person with no appeal against the decision that he be deported.

Chapter Five

Procedures for Dealing with Emergencies

5.1 MPs and stop orders

The various emergency situations that may arise have been outlined in chapter 4. In dealing with many of these situations there is, as Brian Spiro has written, "little time regardless of the legal merits of the case, before the threatened sanction will be operated and the person can no longer be assisted". In such circumstances, the intervention of a Member of Parliament or Peer of the Realm is indispensable. The role of MPs in immigration emergencies is now well established, and, indeed, is seemingly viewed by the Home Office as an integral part of the system.

Every MP has the right to contact the Minister of State responsible for immigration (or, if the MP is a Privy Councillor, the Home Secretary) and request that a "stop order" be placed on the action of the Executive authority. Therefore, in a situation such as an imminent deportation, or removal of an illegal entrant or person refused leave to enter, an MP (or the MP's secretary) should be telephoned, briefly informed of the facts, and asked to place a "stop". Such a request by an MP is invariably complied with (there are standing instructions to this effect) on the understanding that full, written "representations" concerning the matter will shortly be sent by, or via, the member. ("Representations" are fully considered at 5.3, below.) The function of a "stop order" is therefore the limited, but invaluable, one of gaining time.

If the adviser experiences difficulties in contacting an MP, the Immigration Service should nevertheless be told that the intervention of an MP is being sought. Time will normally be given for this purpose.

It is the accepted practice to contact an MP in whose constituency the client has lived, or, if s/he has only recently landed, the MP for the constituency in which his or her relatives or friends reside. (There may, of course, be connections with more than one constituency so that there is a choice of whom to approach.) If for some reason the constituency MP cannot be located, the adviser should approach another member whom s/he feels will be sympathetic, explain the difficulty and request that they intercede and place a "stop". The follow up work including written representations should normally be conducted through their presently unavailable colleague.

The interest which MPs take in matters of immigration seems to vary according to their personal inclinations and the size of ethnic minority groups in their area. They possess total discretion as to whether or not they should take up a case, and adopt no uniform criteria as to the circumstances in which they will do so. While some MPs are nearly always prepared to act, others, for various reasons, are more selective about the case in which they choose to intervene. Some MPs discriminate on the basis that they do not wish to burden the Minister's time with cases they see as unmeritorious, while others fear that if they back weak cases their credibility will be damaged as regards any future dealings with the Home Office. Therefore, the legal representative must often seek to persuade the MP that it is a case in which it is appropriate for him or her to act, and be prepared to give reasons for this belief.

If the case is one that should be taken up but the constituency MP is not prepared to intervene, then s/he should be informed that assistance will be sought elsewhere. If another person is then approached s/he should be informed of the other's refusal. It is a breach not only of etiquette but also of parliamentary privilege if an MP becomes involved in a case arising from another's constituency where the MP for that constituency is willing to act. The second MP may first wish to contact his or her colleague to ensure that the constituency MP has no objections to his or her involvement. The authors have experience of cases "turned down" by a constituency representative, on the ground that it is without hope, later being brought to a successful conclusion after securing the co-operation of another MP.

It was earlier mentioned that Members of the House of Lords as well as the Commons have the power to place a "stop". There are many Peers who take a close interest in the field of immigration and who are quite prepared to provide assistance to individuals where necessary. They are generally undervalued and underused. If a constituency MP is unavailable, serious consideration should be given to asking a sympathetic Peer to procure a "stop", and possibly requesting him or her to be the channel for subsequent representations to the Minister. Furthermore, during the period after a general election has been called and the Commons dissolved, there are literally no MPs in existence who can be approached for help, and at such a time one can only rely on a Member of the Lords.

The number of the House of Commons and Lords switchboard is given at appendix 2.

As has been indicated, an MP or Peer is not only essential in preventing the removal of a client, but is additionally the avenue through which "representations" should be made to the Home Office. Their role in this respect is considered at 5.3, below. That section also considers the situation where there is intervention by several MPs on the same matter.

5.2 Temporary admission, temporary release and bail

(a) Temporary admission

"Temporary admission" is used in the context of port of entry cases. A passenger who is on temporary admission is, under the written authority of an IO (see the IS 96 at appendix 1 group G), allowed physically to enter the UK (subject to restrictions described below) but has *not* been granted "leave to enter" (s11(1)).

The Immigration Service asserts that temporary admission is not used as an alternative to formal leave to enter but only as an alternative to detention. However, one can appreciate how everyone (clients, lawyers, officials etc) involved in immigration law can, on occasion, view it in terms of the authorities wishing to keep a "firmer" control over persons about whom it has doubts.

The Act states that an IO may decide to grant temporary admission to persons detained or liable to detention (Sch 2 para 21(1)). This means that a person may be released on temporary admission either pre-decision pending enquiries, after a decision has been made but before removal, or post-decision but before an appeal hearing (where the right of appeal is exercisable in the UK).

Following the stated policy of the Immigration Service to avoid holding passengers in detention whenever possible, at present IOs tend to exercise their discretion with regard to temporary admission in a relatively generous manner. Indeed, the standing instructions issued to IOs state that:

> "Temporary admission should be readily granted to any person who can be trusted to comply with its terms. In other circumstances it may be used liberally where because of factors such as age, infirmity, sex, close relationship or other compassionate features it is considered that close custody is unnecessary or inappropriate."

Certainly, over the last few years the use of temporary admission as an alternative to detention has increased dramatically. This is well illustrated by the following statistics:

Year	*Passengers granted temporary admission*	*Percentage of passengers refused entry given temporary admission*
1977	2,868	22%
1978	3,874	25%
1979	4,742	23%
1980	5,864	33%
1981	5,776	44%
1982	6,584	54%
1983	7,292	52%
1984	8,527	49%

An IO will not grant temporary admission where s/he feels that there is a danger, if s/he does so, that the person will not observe the restrictions imposed, ie will abscond. (It should be noted that despite the increase in the numbers released on temporary admission the percentage of passengers who have absconded has never risen above 2.1 per cent.)

If the IO is reluctant to release the passenger, the legal adviser must try to persuade him or her to do so as a matter of priority. One must seek to allay doubts by pointing out facts that would appear to indicate the likelihood that any conditions imposed would be obeyed, for example, the existence of a "sponsor" who is willing to provide accommodation.

If the IO is firm in his or her refusal to release the passenger, one should take the matter to the CIO. The assistance of an MP might also be sought.

If one's representations relating to temporary admission are to no avail, it should be noted that, at least where a person has been detained without a decision having been made, after seven days there is an opportunity to apply for bail (see para *(c)*, below).

While a person is in the UK on temporary admission s/he can be subject to any restrictions as to residence and as to reporting to the police or immigration authorities as the IO thinks fit (Sch 2 para 21(2)).

Although temporary admission granted by an IO will usually be for a period of a few days only (ie time sufficient to reach a decision or for removal directions to be finalised), if more time is then needed, further "extensions" will be made. However, if a stop order is obtained and representations made to the Minister, or if an appeal (exercisable from the UK) is lodged, then a longer period of temporary admission or "open" temporary admission will generally be granted.

If a person has been given a period of temporary admission which is about to expire, (that is, the notice states s/he should soon report back to the immigration authorities at the port), then one should telephone the relevant IO *the day before*, and enquire whether the client's presence is really necessary. It may well be that *no* final decision has yet been reached and that a further period of temporary admission can be agreed, in which case a new written notice confirming those details will be sent to the client through the post. Alternatively, it may be that a decision *has* been reached (either by the IO at first instance, or by the Minister considering representations) and that it is intended to remove the passenger the next day. Clearly neither the client nor the adviser would wish removal to be arranged without warning. However, this sometimes happens because Minsters' decisions are sent to the MP through whom representations were made and, occasionally, the MP's office may be rather slow in forwarding a copy to the client or adviser.

The notice invariably requires that the person report back to the port of entry. However, if the person is staying in another part of the country and consults a local adviser, that adviser should telephone the IO at the port of entry and try to persuade him or her to transfer the papers to a more convenient local port to enable subsequent interviews to take place there.

A person on temporary admission can be re-detained at any time (Sch 2 para 21(1)). However, this is not likely to occur unless s/he breaches the conditions imposed.

If it is desired that the client reside elsewhere than at the address stipulated in the notice or if some event, such as illness, prevents him or her reporting on a set day, the immigration authorities should immediately be informed.

(b) Temporary release

Whereas temporary *admission* is concerned with the unofficial admission into the UK of persons who have run into immigration problems on arrival, temporary *release* concerns the discretionary release of persons already in the UK but liable to eventual removal as deportees or illegal entrants.

(i) Deportation

POWER TO DETAIN OR RELEASE

Persons in respect of whom a court has recommended deportation, persons against whom a *decision* to deport has been taken, and persons against whom a deportation *order* has been made have been considered in chapter 4.2 paras *(d)–(f)*. Any of these persons may be detained or released by the Secretary of State (Sch 3 para 2(1)–(3) respectively). Regarding deportation recommendations, efforts will already have been made by a solicitor/barrister to obtain a direction for release from the sentencing court (Sch 3 para 2(1)) or from the court considering any appeal against the recommendation (Sch 3 para 2(1A)). In so doing, Home Office Circular No 133/1978, dated 12 July 1978, will hopefully have been brought to the attention of the court. That circular reminds the courts that, in the absence of an express direction for release, detention will follow and that, when considering release, the provisions of the Bail Act 1976 should be borne in mind (see appendix 3).

CONDITIONS

Where the Secretary of State allows temporary release under Sch 3 para 2(1)–(3), that release may be unconditional or may be subject to "such restrictions as to *residence* and as to *reporting to the police* as may from time to time be notified . . . in writing by the Secretary of State" (Sch 3 para 2(5) (emphasis supplied)). Where, on recommending deportation, a court directs release, that release may also be subject to the same conditions (Sch 3 para 4) and the court may at any later stage vary those conditions whether on an immigration officer's application or on an application made by or on behalf of the prospective deportee (Sch 3 para 5).

Breach of a condition imposed by a court may result in arrest without warrant by a constable or an IO (Sch 3 para 7) but there is no power of arrest in respect of a breach of conditions imposed by the Secretary of State. Really, there is no need for such a power in that the Secretary of State may simply revoke temporary release.

CUSTODIAL SENTENCE

Where a person recommended for deportation is also serving a custodial sentence, then, unless the court directed release (upon completion of the sentence) or unless the Secretary of State has so directed, detention under the 1971 Act will follow the custodial sentence. Accordingly, efforts to obtain temporary release from the Secretary of State should be made *well before* the sentence finishes. If no recommendation has been made, there is no liability to detention unless the Secretary of State in the meanwhile decides to make a deportation order under s3(5)(b)—an order for detention may then be made under Sch 3 para 2(2) (see chapter 4.2 paras *(c)–(e)*). In such cases bail may be applied for once notice of appeal against the decision has been given (see below).

(ii) *Illegal entrants*

POWER TO DETAIN OR RELEASE

Chapter 4.2 (paras *(g)* and *(h)*) considers persons who have been arrested or detained as suspected illegal entrants and persons in respect of whom that suspicion has been established to the satisfaction of the immigration authorities (in practice this usually means form IS 151 A has been served). Whereas deportation matters are the concern of the Secretary of State (ie the appropriate Group within the IND at Croydon), illegal entry cases are the responsibility of the Immigration Service. Once treated as an illegal entrant, detention pending removal from the UK may follow (Sch 2 para 16(2)). However, with the written authority of an IO, temporary release may be granted (Sch 2 para 21(1)).

CONDITIONS

Where an IO authorises temporary release, that release may be unconditional or may be subject to "such restrictions as to *residence* and as to *reporting to the police or an immigration office* as may from time to time be notified . . . in writing by an immigration officer" (Sch 2 para 21(2) (emphasis supplied)).

There is no express power of arrest for such a breach but being granted temporary release "shall not prejudice a later exercise of the power to detain" (Sch 2 para 21(1)) so the temporary release may simply be terminated.

CUSTODIAL SENTENCE

Where the recipient of an IS 151 A is completing a custodial sentence, then completion of it will immediately be followed by detention under the Immigration Act pending eventual removal. Temporary release from an IO should be sought *well before* completion of the custodial sentence.

(iii) *Place of detention* Persons detained under the administrative provisions of the 1971 Act are treated in all respects as remand prisoners; that is to say, unconvicted persons remanded in custody. Some (especially persons arrested as illegal entrants or on the basis of an outstanding deportation order) may spend the first few hours of detention, or the first night or two, in the local police station. In London, men will usually be transferred to the Deport Block at Ashford Remand Centre, Middlesex, and women to the remand wing of HMP Holloway. Further, alleged illegal entrants (both men and women) are often detained at the Harmondsworth Detention Centre near Heathrow. Outside the London area the place of detention will usually be the remand wing of the local prison.

(iv) *Obtaining temporary release*

PRELIMINARIES

Before requesting temporary release contact with the appropriate authority will of course be necessary in that the full facts of the case will have to be ascertained or confirmed. Further, if at all possible the detainee should be visited so that instructions may be obtained and advice given. Where a case is wholly without merit, the best advice may be to agree to removal rather than to languish for weeks or months in detention. Some detainees may wish to leave the UK as soon as possible *irrespective* of the merits of the case. Voluntary and supervised departures (and how to expedite them) are discussed in 5.7, below; the authorities one may need to contact are set out in appendix 2.

METHOD OF APPROACH

Temporary release is requested by means of oral and/or written representations. Representations and the style they require are considered in 5.3, below. Suffice it here to say that over the telephone or in a letter the case for temporary release should be put as persuasively as possible and with reference to any favourable facts.

WHO TO APPROACH

Where the detainee is awaiting the making or execution of a *deportation order*, one must approach the Home Office in Croydon. Generally, resort to written representations may be necessary as it is difficult to make telephone contact and within the IND such contact appears to be discouraged. Written representations should usually be sent to the Under Secretary of State, IND, Lunar House, but if the Home Office reference number is not known, then it is better to send the representations direct to the Deportations Machinery Group, IND, Lunar House.

Where the detainee is being treated as an *illegal entrant*, one must contact the caseworker section of the local Immigration Service office. In London this will usually be the Harmondsworth Intelligence Unit or Isis House in Southwark. The IO or CIO will usually be responsible for the case and willing to listen to oral representations made by telephone or in person. If the IO or CIO does not grant temporary release, one may then aim higher in the Immigration Service hierarchy (see pp8–9) and direct written representations to the Assistant Chief Inspector with a copy to the IO or CIO responsible for the case.

FLEXIBILITY OF TEMPORARY RELEASE REPRESENTATIONS

It must be emphasised that no rules of law dictate the way oral or written representations should be directed. Nor is there any rigidity concerning the precise moment at which representations should be made or the exact officer to whom those representations should be made or what they should contain. Representations are simply a device which seek to persuade an immigration authority to exercise a discretion vested in that authority by the 1971 Act—practitioners should be aware of the device and of the authority possessing the discretion. Beyond that, each person should develop his or her own rules of practice. The precise moment at which to make representations is usually governed by urgency. Other than that, some practitioners prefer oral representations to written; some prefer approaching higher grade officers to lower; some make "one off" representations only while others prefer repetition; some never use an MP whereas others invariably do, or progress from a direct approach to an approach through an MP. One must establish one's own technique and often a given individual's practices will differ depending on the nature and circumstances of the case. Clearly, absolute rules cannot be laid down when it comes to the making of representations except to say that representations requesting temporary release must, where deportation is involved, be directed to the Home Office in Croydon whereas representations in respect of illegal entrants should in the first instance be made to the IO or CIO at the casework section of the appropriate Immigration Service office.

CONTENTS OF REPRESENTATIONS

Of course, the facts contained in representations will differ from case to case. One should try, however, to pay particular attention to the following:

(a) risk of detainee absconding;
(b) fixed address at which to live;
(c) presence of friends/relatives in locality or at fixed address;
(d) immigration record of friends/relatives;
(e) continuing studies;
(f) medical/compassionate considerations;
(g) length of residence in the UK;
(h) extent to which detainee is established in the UK;
(i) matters relevant to detainee's credibility;
(j) how far off eventual removal may be.

The Secretary of State has conceded that the immigration authorities will not necessarily be aware of all relevant facts (Home Office Circular No 113/1978 para 3). Indeed, where an authority changes its mind and decides to grant temporary release, it saves face if facts have been disclosed which were not known previously.

Finally, if necessary, reference may be made to the finding of law that a person may properly be detained pending removal only if that removal will occur within a *reasonable period*; where removal will not take place reasonably quickly, the power to detain must not be exercised (*Hardial Singh* (1983) 13 December (unreported), DC *per* Woolf J).

(c) Immigration bail

Certain passengers who have been refused temporary admission and certain prospective deportees or illegal entrants who have been refused temporary release may be eligible to apply for immigration bail. Those who may apply are, firstly, passengers who have been detained for seven days without a decision on their leave to enter application having been made (Sch 2 para 22(1)) and, second, passengers and others who have an immigration appeal pending (Sch 2 para 29(1)).

(i) *Passengers at ports of entry* Such persons have two opportunities to apply for bail.

SEVEN DAYS OF DETENTION

A passenger seeking leave to enter who has been detained for seven days without a decision being made may apply to an adjudicator for bail (Sch 2 para 22(1)). Any such passenger must be notified of this right and told that a friend or legal adviser may be contacted to assist with the bail application (HC 169 para 88). Seven days' detention without a decision is a situation which rarely arises. See also below.

PENDING AN APPEAL

Once refused entry, a passenger may have an appeal (exercisable from within the UK) against the decision that leave is required, the refusal of leave, or the destination to which s/he is to be removed (Sch 2 para 29(1); see appeals and time limits chart on pp38–39, above). The passenger may apply for bail once such an appeal is pending. This is discussed further below.

(ii) *Before any deportation decision is made* Such persons will generally not yet be at the stage where they may be detained except, that is, for persons who have been arrested, charged and convicted of an offence. In such cases, only criminal bail may be available, as well as court bail pending any appeal against conviction or sentence (see also p33, above).

(iii) *Once a deportation decision has been made* Except for decisions taken in pursuance of a court recommendation, a decision to make a deportation order may almost always be appealed within the immigration system (see chapter 4.2 paras *(d)* and *(e)*). If temporary admission/release has been refused, bail may be applied for once a deportation appeal is *pending* (Sch 3 para 3; Sch 2 para 29(1)). (This is discussed further below.)

(iv) *Once a deportation order has been made* As can be seen from the appeals and time limits chart on pp38–39, a prospective deportee may appeal against the destination to which s/he is to be removed, though usually such an appeal will be brought at the same time as the appeal against the decision itself. However, in the few circumstances in which a *separate* destination appeal may be brought after the making of an order, bail may be applied for pending that appeal (Sch 3 para 3; Sch 2 para 29(1)). It is immaterial whether or not in accordance with Sch 3 para 3 and Sch 2 para 30(1) the Secretary of State consents to bail (*Alghali* [1984] Imm AR 106, QBD). See also, below.

(v) *Alleged illegal entrants* Insofar as alleged illegal entrants have a right of appeal exercisable from within the UK against the validity of removal directions, or against the destination specified in those directions (see the chart on pp38–39, above), an application for bail may be made pending any such appeal (Sch 2 para 29(1)). Again, it is immaterial whether or not in accordance with Sch 2 para 30(1) the Secretary of State consents (*Alghali*, above). See also, below.

(vi) *Applying for bail*

SEVEN DAY DETAINEES

Passengers detained for seven days without a decision being made may apply *only* to an appellate authority (Sch 2 para 22(1)). See below.

PENDING AN APPEAL

There are two levels at which bail may be requested pending an appeal: first, bail may be granted by a chief immigration officer or police inspector (Sch 2 para 29(1) and (2)) or, second, bail may be granted by an appellate authority (Sch 2 para 29(3) and (4)). Accordingly, as soon as notice of appeal is given (see chapter 5.5, below), one should apply to the appropriate chief immigration officer or police inspector. This is done *orally* (Procedure Rules 1984 r23(1)(a)); that is to say, the request for bail may be made in person or over the phone. The appellant may then be bailed upon entering into his or her own recognisance, and s/he will be required to appear before the appellate authorities at a specified time and place.

If the CIO or police inspector refuses bail, application may then be made to the appellate authorities (Sch 2 para 29(3) and (4); see below).

APPLYING TO THE APPELLATE AUTHORITIES

Once temporary admission/release has been refused and (under the "pending appeal" provisions) once bail from a CIO or police inspector has been attempted, application for bail may then be made to the appellate authorities (Sch 2 para 29(3)). The application may be made orally or in writing (Procedure Rules 1984 r23(1)(b)). One is advised to apply *orally* in that only at an oral hearing can one deal with any objections to bail that may be raised. Accordingly, the nearest Immigration Appeals Centre should be telephoned and a hearing date requested (see appendix 2). It may well be several days before a hearing takes place—one reason for this is that the appellate authorities may have to confirm that notice of appeal has been given (ie that an appeal is pending). The adjudicator may then bail the *passenger* or *appellant* on his or her entering into a recognisance (Sch 2 paras 22(1) and 29(3) respectively); conditions which appear likely to result in the appearance of the passenger or appellant at the required time and place may be imposed, and sureties may be required (Sch 2 paras 22(2) and 29(5)). Prior to any hearing, the names, addresses and occupations of two persons who might act as sureties should be obtained (Procedure Rules 1984 r23(2)(e)) and one should ensure that their immigration history and status is sound. Bail may otherwise be granted subject to sureties being obtained and taken at a later stage (Sch 2 paras 22(3) and 29(6)).

Although the Bail Act 1976 does not apply to immigration bail, the principles and arguments are similar and anyone who has applied for bail in a criminal matter will generally be quite at home applying for bail before an adjudicator (see also para *(b)*(iv), above, on the contents of representations). If an appeal is pending, the merits of that appeal should not be material.

Finally, there is no appeal against an adjudicator's refusal to grant bail. One may, however, reapply. Where an appeal pending before an adjudicator ultimately goes to the Tribunal (see chapter 4.4 para *(b)*(iii)), a fresh bail application is advised in that it will then be considered by the Tribunal.

5.3 Representations

(a) Introduction
"Representations" (that is, the conveying of information to the immigration authorities in order to persuade them to follow a particular course of action), can be undertaken at various times and for various reasons.

The making of representations will arise in some cases where the right of appeal through the tribunals and courts has been exhausted, in others representations will be made additionally or in the alternative to proceedings before the appellate authorities, and in others where there is either no right of appeal at all or at least none existing while the person remains in the UK.

The use of representations in seeking temporary admission or release has already been mentioned (see 5.2, above). The more general use of representations in emergency situations will now be considered.

(b) Representations made before a decision has been reached
It is sometimes profitable to make representations, either orally or in writing, to the authorities *before* a decision has been taken. Indeed, representations discussing the substance of the case may well be made at the same time as, and incorporating, submissions concerning temporary admission or release.

There is no rigidity with regard to the precise moment at which representations concerning the substantive merits of the case should be made, what they should contain, or to whom they should be directed. However, in practice, where no decision has yet been reached with respect to a passenger seeking entry, representations (be they oral or written) are usually directed to the particular IO dealing with the case. Similarly, representations regarding persons threatened with removal from the UK as illegal entrants, or as prospective deportees, should be directed to the appropriate Immigration Service Office or to the Home Office in Croydon, respectively. Alternatively, (particularly in the case of persons in the UK faced with possible removal) one may feel the need to make representations, even at this pre-decision stage, via an MP, direct to the Minister. It can only be reiterated that the precise route one should take depends on the nature and circumstances of the case.

It is up to the legal representative to prepare arguments and to produce the appropriate evidence that a person should be allowed to remain or be admitted for the purpose for which entry is sought. It is imperative that relevant information should be forwarded to the authorities so that their decision is based on the full facts.

The importance of making representations at the pre-decision stage is often not fully appreciated. The Home Office at Croydon and the IO at Heathrow or elsewhere, possess considerable *discretion* in the exercise of their duty. One must seek to persuade them to exercise that discretion in the client's favour.

Immigration officers, for example, regularly exercise discretion both "within" and "outside" the Immigration Rules. One of the many examples of where discretion is visibly exercised within the Rules can be illustrated by reference to HC 169 para 83, which states that a passenger convicted of an offence listed as an extraditable crime is to be refused *unless* the IO considers admission to be justified for "strong compassionate reasons". The Rules do not define "strong compassionate reasons", thus leaving it open to the passenger to persuade the IO that the circumstances of his or her particular case warrant admission. (Of course the "Secret Instructions" referred to at chapter 4.1 para *(b)*, above, elaborate the Rules and together with relevant caselaw, may well have a strong bearing on the eventual decision reached.)

Discretion may be exercised favourably even in respect of Rules which are unambiguous and would seem to allow no leeway. An example of such discretion being exercised totally outside of the Rules is provided with reference to HC 169 para 10. This states that visa nationals *must* have a visa issued for the purpose for which they seek entry, and leave *shall* be refused if this is not produced. Nevertheless, it is well known that IOs sometimes grant entry where there are particular reasons for doing so, such as the existence of compassionate circumstances prompting urgent travel, or a genuine case of misunderstanding or misinformation supplied to the passenger. In such cases, the passenger may be allowed in with a warning.

The discretion retained by IOs is part of the general discretion retained in the hands of the Executive (and referred to, albeit impliedly, in s19(1)). The Home Secretary has the power to waive the Rules for an individual's benefit, and this power may also be exercised by Home Office officials acting in his name.

As Harlow and Rawlings have written:

> "All the actors concerned (pressure groups, adjudicators, officials etc) work on the basis that Ministers can and sometimes will depart from the Rules. When restructuring the scheme, government saw this as a key component, importing, according to Mr Rees (HC SCA 1968/9 cols 69–78), the necessary flexibility and political responsibility. The Department can exercise compassion in individual 'hard' cases."

Following this reasoning, even the giving of indefinite leave to a passenger by an IO who has no authority within the Rules to do so, is valid and binding on the Home Office (*Ram* [1979] 1 WLR 148). However, the situation is of course quite different if the passenger indulged in deception in order to acquire such leave. It should be mentioned that, naturally, IOs have *no* discretion to give the Rules a *narrower* interpretation than is proper (*Kharrazi* [1980] 1 WLR 1396).

(c) Representations made after a decision has been reached

If the authorities have made a decision to refuse leave to enter, to deport or to remove, one should usually seek to have a "stop order" placed (see 5.1, above), on the understanding that written representations are to follow quickly. (The Immigration Service chase up MPs who have caused stop orders to be imposed but who have failed quickly to forward representations.)

The Home Secretary's discretion (see above) means that an executive decision can be reversed either on the grounds of a change of policy or, as is far more common, on a "one-off" basis.

Schedule 2 para 6(3) of the Act states that a person who has been given a notice refusing leave to enter may at any time have that notice cancelled by a further notice in writing given to him or her by the IO (see appendix 1 group A). However, it should be stressed that, irrespective of who initially made the decision, once the decision has been made the representations should always be sent (via the MP) to the *Minister of State*.

The person to prepare these formal representations should be the client's legal adviser rather than the MP or Peer. To prepare full representations properly would take up a disproportionate amount of an MP's time, and might possibly discourage him or her from agreeing to act in a similar case in the future. Furthermore, the representations, if left entirely in the hands of an MP, however enthusiastic, may well not be up to the standard of those prepared by a legal practitioner with experience of immigration and knowledge of the intricacies of the law. Brian Spiro is surely accurate when he states: "The MP [should] act more as a means to access to the Minister rather than as an actual case-worker".

One should therefore send written representations to the MP and ask him or her to forward these to the Minister, together with any additional comments that s/he would care to make. (Incidentally, sometimes, after the initial representations have been submitted, a further piece of information or documentary evidence may need to be forwarded to the Minister. The legal adviser should also send this via the MP and *not* direct to Queen Anne's Gate.)

The contents of the written representations will generally be a mixture of law and fact, the precise ratio depending upon the particular case. It should be understood that in the emergency situations described in this book the adviser will not have the benefit of seeing "explanatory statements" prepared by the authorities containing the alleged comments of the client at interview and detailing the reasons for Home Office actions. Unfortunately, this means that the adviser must often make an inspired guess as to, for example, what prompted a refusal of leave to enter, and as to precisely what are the most crucial points to concentrate on in making the submission.

A typical representation, taken from an actual case is shown at appendix 1. This case is in fact a perfect example of much that has been discussed both in this chapter and in chapter 4.1, above. The person arrived at a port of entry and on the same day was refused leave to enter on the ground that a deportation order was in force against him (HC 169 para 84). He was granted temporary admission while arrangements were made for his removal. At this stage he sought legal advice. The constituency MP was requested to place a "stop order" but declined to do so on the ground that the Minister would never reverse such a decision. A member of the Lords was then approached, a "stop order" obtained, the client's temporary admission extended, and representations channeled to the Minister. Some weeks later, the Minister, exercising his discretion exceptionally, revoked the deportation order and granted leave to enter.

In recent years, Ministers for Immigration have become agitated by the frequency of representations by successive members concerning the same case. The present Minister, Mr Waddington, on 14 July 1983 sent a letter to all MPs stating what remains his attitude. (This letter is fully reproduced at appendix 1.) Essentially, the Minister states that he will give detailed consideration to the *first* representations that he receives from whoever may send them, be they an MP or a Peer. However, if it is apparent that these representations do not come from the constituency MP, but that the constituency member can be readily identified, s/he will be approached and given the opportunity to comment if s/he wishes to do so.

The letter goes on to state that, generally speaking, "stays on decisions" taken after the first representations have been considered (and rejected) will not be made unless there are significant new facts. Although the wording of this letter is not totally clear, it would seem that once the Minister has considered and rejected representations, the intervention of other members reiterating the same facts will not normally prevent removals. However, the making of second representations by the same MP, if justified, after the Minister's initial rejection does often result in a further stay on removal while the case is again reviewed.

The making of representations in port of entry emergencies was recently discussed at length in the House of Commons. On 25 October 1985 Mr Waddington stated:

> "Arrangements are not working as well as they might, because some MPs are abusing their right to make representations. Recently cases have come to my attention where MPs have invited people to come (to the UK), knowing that they have no claim to entry, telling them that they have only to mention the MP's name and temporary admission will be obtained. It is highly unsatisfactory. . . . In 1980 representations were made by MPs in 1,000 cases. In 1985, we estimate that representations will have been made in 4,500 cases. . . . An enormous burden has been placed on the immigration and nationality department. It does not lie in the mouth of MPs to say there ought to be more staff unless they are prepared to address themselves to the fact that something is wrong with the system because some MPs, and I am not afraid to use the word, are abusing the system."

Mr Waddington's rather emotive comments created a political storm. In particular, Opposition MPs demanded that the Minister name those responsible for "abusing" the system.

On 30 October 1985, Mr Hurd, the Home Secretary, gave further details to the Commons:

> "Home Office Ministers received representations on immigration cases about 20 times a week in 1980. Last year the average was some 70 a week. In the past few weeks there have been 200 representations a week. I must make it clear that the increase since 1980 is not the result of some dramatic change in the criteria being employed by immigration officers at the ports in operating the immigration rules. Nor can it be explained by an increase in

> passenger traffic which has increased by 25 per cent while MPs' representations have increased five-fold taking the year as a whole. Members are being approached and asked to put 'stops' on cases more often than in the past and members are agreeing to ask for 'stops' on cases more often than in the past. This interest has created real administrative problems for the staff at ports."

However, it is significant that Mr Waddington further commented that the system whereby MPs could make representations was "perfectly reasonable, provided that MPs are prepared to operate it in a sensible and responsible fashion". Similarly, Mr Hurd expressly remarked that he believed that the "present system suits both our geography and our constitution". He stressed that his remarks (quoted above) were made in order to prompt a discussion as to how the existing procedure could best operate, and asked the House to accept that the Government wished to make "a genuine attempt to strike the right balance . . . between the representations of MPs and the need for an effective and efficient control without the strains at present imposed on it".

It would be extremely difficult politically for any government to remove the fundamental right of MPs and Peers to request stop orders and to make representations on matters they consider to be of importance. Any implication that the Government wished to restrict this right would be strongly criticised as constitutionally improper. Indeed, Mr Kaufman said to the Commons on 30 October 1985 that the recent Government allegations were not more than "a whine that the actions of MPs are inconvenient to the Executive".

After written representations have been sent to the Minister, the emergency situation can be said for the moment to have passed. It is the authors' experience that several weeks, or indeed months, will go by before the Minister reaches a decision on the matter. In fact the time gained by the "stop" will, if the passenger was seeking entry to the UK only for a holiday, sometimes be a victory in itself as long as the person is released on temporary admission/release. The authors have experienced cases where the client has long since departed from the country by the time a decision has been reached. However, it is still desirable to purge what would otherwise remain a stain on the client's immigration record—capable of prejudicing future dealings with the immigration authorities—if it is at all possible.

It is outside the scope of this book to consider fully in what circumstances there is "likely" to be a reversal of the initial decision, but the point should be made that individual Home Secretaries and Ministers of State have differed in their attitudes quite considerably. Furthermore, the approach of individual Ministers can "harden" or "relax" the attitudes of IOs and the Home Office as a whole. For example, the administration of Robert Carr was noted for its "robust" attitude and the fact that passengers refused entry were invariably detained, while the Home Secretaryship of Roy Jenkins liberally allowed temporary admission and was far more inclined to sympathetic consideration of individual cases on their merits. Even in more recent years, practitioners noted a hardening in attitudes between the regime of William Whitelaw (and Timothy Raison) and that of Leon Brittan (and David Waddington).

A letter from the previous Home Secretary, Mr Brittan, replying to the representations of an MP stated:

> "I know you recognise that I have a responsibility to act fairly towards those applicants who do observe the proper procedures, and that only in the most exceptional circumstances would I be justified in setting aside the normal requirements of the Immigration Rules. . . . the passenger's misrepresentations to secure entry to the UK . . . weigh heavily against affording him such favourable treatment."

There is a strong desire for "truth" in the approach of the Home Office, and if the client has attempted to deceive—even on matters of little significance in themselves—this is often fatal if one later seeks to persuade ministerial discretion to be exercised. This is so unfortunately even in cases where, undeniably, compassionate circumstances exist.

5.4 Campaigns

Many commentators have noted that in recent years there has been a marked increase in the formation of "immigration campaigns". Although hybrids exist, campaigns are essentially of two types: those that agitate for change in aspects of general immigration law and practice; and those that are formed around individual cases in the hope of influencing their outcome.

In practice, the majority of campaigns have related to persons living inside the UK who are threatened with removal by deportation, or as alleged illegal entrants. However, campaigns are launched occasionally on behalf of persons who are refused leave to enter at a port (the case most readily springing to mind being that of Afia Begum, who was released on temporary admission before going to ground).

The initiation of a campaign may therefore be among the procedures considered when an emergency arises. However, it should be a procedure adopted *in addition to*, for example, the making of representations to the Minister, rather than as an *alternative* to any of the procedures discussed above. What will be involved in a campaign must be fully explained to the client, and their consent obtained before any action is taken.

In fact, one can lay down no set rules either regarding the type of case that "can" be launched into a campaign, or about the tactics to be adopted by a campaigning organisation (although some suggestions are given below). Obviously, a private solicitors' firm will not have the resources to undertake campaigning (although certain law centres may be able and willing to do so). Nevertheless, legal advisers should remain in close contact with the activists involved in such a campaign, and indeed may encourage its formation and development. It is essential that a number of persons commit themselves to act as the co-ordinators of any campaign, and to ensure that continued pressure will be applied to the Home Office over what may be a long period of time.

The tactics adopted by a campaign will depend entirely on the circumstances of the particular case. The local MP (who may already be involved in the case, see 5.1 and 5.3, above), should be asked for his or her support, as should local and national organisations (such as trade unions, ethnic minority associations, etc). One should attempt to obtain maximum publicity for the case by ensuring involvement of the media (local and national newspapers and, if possible, television). The use of petitions, leaflets, demonstrations and much else can and should be adopted during the campaign. Advice concerning the setting up and running of campaigns can be obtained from various of the organisations listed in appendix 2.

Although assessing the value of campaigns in influencing the outcome of individual cases is very difficult, applying pressure to the Minister at the time when he is considering the case is generally considered to be a useful exercise.

5.5 Making applications and bringing appeals

(a) The operation of applications and appeals

Both applications and appeals may be necessary devices with which to deal with a possible emergency, and in any event will probably be essential to the client's interest. An application to the Secretary of State on behalf of an overstayer may pre-empt a decision to deport that person (see chapter 4.2 para *(d)*) and bringing an appeal against the destination specified in removal directions may prevent imminent removal from the UK (see chapter 4.2 para *(h)*).

Quite apart from applications and appeals being used as devices, a *separate* emergency may exist in relation to the making of an application or bringing of an appeal itself (see chapter 4.4).

How to make an application, bring an appeal and deal with any time limit problem in respect of either, is considered in the following paragraphs.

(b) Making applications

(i) *How to apply and to whom* Applications for an extension or variation made by a person who is already in the UK must be directed to the Under Secretary of State, IND, Lunar House in that all such applications are considered in the name of the Secretary of State. A standard application form exists (the RON 52) but it is little used and one is advised, instead, simply to apply in writing by means of a letter. Applications for entry clearance by persons outside the UK must usually be made to the nearest British post (HC 169 para 12) and will be considered by the entry clearance officer (telephone the Foreign and Commonwealth Office for the address (see appendix 2)). Various standard and local application forms exist (for example, the standard yellow IM2 for most Commonwealth citizens) but, again, a simple letter will initially suffice.

As a matter of law, any written letter of application (whether to the Secretary of State or to an entry clearance officer) will be properly made so long as it contains "a request in quite unambiguous terms for an [entry clearance] to be issued to a particular person" (*Brown* [1976] Imm AR 119).

(ii) *Contents of an application* The above quote from *Brown's case* indicates the minimum content of an application (eg "I apply on behalf of X for a three-month extension of his leave to remain as a visitor"). This may be referred to as a "holding" application—it meets the test laid down in *Brown's case* and the factual details and relevant documentation can follow later once expert advice, if necessary, has been obtained.

(iii) *When an application is "made"* An application is "made" on the day on which it is personally given to the appropriate immigration authority or, if posted, on the day on which it is put into the post (*Lubetkin* [1979–80] Imm AR 162). Accordingly, where a time limit is involved, it need not be *received* by the deadline. However, if the deadline falls on a day when there is no postal collection, the application will be post-marked the following day and so will be out of time (*Petrou* [1978] Imm AR 87, where it was held that no regard can be had to Sundays and public holidays).

(iv) *Methods of conveying an application* No method is prescribed other than that, as a matter of practice, the application should generally be in a written format. Time permitting, a letter is of course the obvious method to use. Letters may be sent by registered, recorded or ordinary delivery. However, where the time limit has practically expired, personal delivery should be considered and, indeed, there is nothing to prevent a "holding" application being made by telemessage or telex. One may dial 100 and ask for British Telecom's telex service and a telex will be sent immediately. The telex numbers of British posts abroad can be obtained from the Foreign and Commonwealth Office (see appendix 2).

(v) *Who may make an application?* As a matter of practice, applications directed to the Secretary of State may be made by the applicant or by a person acting on his or her behalf. The practice of entry clearance officers, however, differs from post to post—some require the signature of the applicant (or of the applicant's parent/guardian) whereas others will be satisfied with an application made by a representative (see also chapter 4.4 para *(b)*(i)).

(c) Bringing appeals

(i) *The need to know* The system of immigration appeals is considered briefly in chapter 4.4 above, and the principal rights of appeal are given in the chart on pp38–39. As indicated above, knowing when and how to initiate appeal proceedings is important for two reasons: first, the discussions of port emergencies and emergencies concerning deportation and illegal entry (chapter 4.1 and 4.2, above) show that at various stages an appeal may be brought either as a serious challenge to a decision of an immigration authority, or as a means of preventing imminent removal, or both. Second, bringing an appeal may secure a client's temporary liberty in that once an appeal is *pending*, a bail application can be made (see 5.2 para *(c)*, above). It is clear, therefore, that dealing with an immigration emergency may well involve the bringing of an appeal.

Alternatively (or additionally), the bringing of an appeal may itself constitute an immigration emergency in that the time limit in which an appeal may be brought may be about to expire.

(ii) *Notice of appeal* Notice of appeal must generally be given in writing to the immigration authority whose decision or action one wishes to appeal; ie an entry clearance officer, an IO or the Secretary of State (Procedure Rules 1984 r6(1) and (2)). Notice may only be given orally where a passenger has been refused entry and has a right of appeal exercisable from within the UK (r6(1)). In such cases the IO, when refusing entry, will explain that an appeal prior to removal is available and will ask the passenger if s/he wishes to initiate proceedings. Giving notice of appeal orally is, therefore, very simple.

Written notice of appeal may be given by means of a letter containing various details relating to the appellant and the appeal which s/he wishes to bring (see below).

The Procedure Rules containing these requirements came into force on 1 March 1985. The rules in force prior to that date simply provided that notice of appeal had to be given by completing a notice of appeal form. This meant that whenever an immigration authority took an appealable decision or action, a blank appeal form would be issued. Despite expectations to the contrary, this procedure did *not* end when the new rules came into force, and private correspondence with the authors confirms that at present there is no intention of discontinuing this practice. Accordingly, procedure law currently gives an appellant a choice: written notice of appeal may be given either in the form of a letter or by completing the blank form issued by the authority whose decision or action is to be appealed (see appendix 1 group F where the three notice of appeal forms are shown—the entry clearance officer's "APP201"; the IO's "IS87"; and the Secretary of State's "APP1").

(iii) *Contents of a notice of appeal* The current Procedure Rules require that notice of appeal given in the form of a letter must, in effect, contain the same information as is requested in the blank appeal forms (r6(3)). That is to say the name, address, date of birth and nationality of the appellant, details of the decision or action being appealed, the ground upon which the appellant intends to rely and (if appropriate) details relating to any destination appeal. Two points in particular should be noted:

(a) one should not worry about detailing the grounds of the appeal in that the appeal is by entitlement so that the grounds can be very short and general (eg "the decision was not in accordance with immigration law and the Rules"). In any event, the grounds may be amplified at the appeal hearing (r6(4)). If in doubt, simply write "grounds to follow" or "grounds to be given at hearing".
(b) where a destination appeal is being brought (either on its own or at the same time as some other appeal), the Procedure Rules require *more*

information than is requested on the blank appeal forms. The appellant's *objections* to the destination must be explained, an *alternative* destination must be specified, and reference must be made to evidence which tends to show that the alternative destination will *admit* the appellant (r6(3) and see HC 169 para 169).

(iv) *When notice of appeal is "given"* Written notice of appeal (be it a letter or completed form) is not "given" until it is *received* by the appropriate immigration authority (*Rocha* [1982] Imm AR 12). The various time limits that apply are shown in the chart on pp38–39. If notice of appeal cannot be given on the day the time limit expires because that day is a Saturday, Sunday or public holiday, it will suffice if it is given on the next working day (r43(1)). In calculating the time limit one starts from the day on which notice of the immigration authority's decision was posted or served in person (r4(11)).

(v) *Method of conveying a notice of appeal* Whenever possible, written notice of appeal should be given by registered, recorded or personal delivery (r44(1)). No other method is specified by the Procedure Rules. However, ordinary postal delivery and emergency methods such as telemessage and telex will nevertheless constitute valid service (*Rocha* [1982] Imm AR 12). The only difference between service in accordance with the Procedure Rules and service not in accordance with them is that the former raises certain presumptions under the Interpretation Act 1978 (*Rocha*, above).

(vi) *Who may give notice of appeal* Written or oral notice of appeal may be given by the appellant, a parent/guardian, or a duly authorised representative (rr6(1) and (5) and 26(2)). The person giving oral notice of appeal must always sign the letter or form (r6(5); and see r8(2)(iii)).

(vii) *Out of time notices* If the appropriate time limit has expired, notice of appeal should still be given as the action *may* be allowed to proceed (r5). This should be done *immediately*, especially where the appeal is against a decision to make a deportation order: no appeal will be possible if the order has already been signed, but if it has *not* been signed the appeal may continue.

(viii) *Applications for leave to appeal from an adjudicator to the Tribunal* Applications for leave are considered briefly in chapter 4.4 para *(b)*(iii). Regarding the making of applications and their contents, paras (ii) and (iii) above apply as they do to notices (except for the changes of terminology); that is to say, the application must generally be in *writing* (r16(1)) though current practice allows an applicant to apply either in the form of a letter or by means of a completed "APP2" (see appendix 1 group F). A blank APP2 form will continue to be issued by the appellate authorities whenever an adjudicator dismisses an appeal. Whether in the form of a letter or an APP2, the application must contain information similar to that contained in a notice of appeal (r16(2); see the APP2 at appendix 1 group F). The same point made in respect of destination appeals applies, except that the *grounds* of the appeal must be expertly drafted or leave may not be granted. In an emergency one should therefore do no more than state "grounds to follow" as extra time will then be given.

The points made in paras (iv)–(vi), above, also apply to applications for leave in the same way as they apply to notices of appeal. The 14-day or 42-day time limit (see chapter 4.4 para *(b)*(iii)) starts to run from the day on which the adjudicator's determination is *received* by the applicant (*Suleman* [1976] Imm AR 147). If the time limit has expired, there is no point making an application as there is no discretion to accept it out of time (*Armstrong* [1977] Imm AR 84).

5.6 Judicial review and habeas corpus

Orders 53 and 54 of the Rules of the Supreme Court relate to the High Court's power to review administrative actions and to issue a writ of habeas corpus (see appendix 3 for further reading).

(a) Habeas corpus

Habeas corpus has been used particularly in the context of illegal entry, in that a writ of habeas corpus requires the detainee to be produced and the reasons for his or her detention to be given. In effect, this procedure may not only secure a detainee's release, but may also constitute a substantive challenge to the decision that s/he is an illegal entrant. For present purposes, habeas corpus proceedings need not be considered in greater detail in that expert assistance will always have to be obtained before such proceedings can be considered.

(b) Judicial review

Judicial review is more commonly resorted to than habeas corpus and it is used to challenge a wide variety of administrative decisions including determinations of adjudicators and the Tribunal. Although such cases must be referred to legal practitioners who are acquainted with review procedure in an immigration context, persons dealing with emergencies have a critical role to play. Quite simply, where emergency assistance is requested by or on behalf of a person who is about to be removed from the UK, that removal may be deferred if the IO at the port is told that one intends to move for judicial review.

Generally, imminent removal should be prevented by means of a stop order (see chapter 5.1, above) followed by representations (see chapter 5.3, above). However, if such procedures have been tried already yet it appears that in responding to the representations the Secretary of State has erred in law, or has been clearly unreasonable, or has based his decision on materially incorrect facts, judicial review should sometimes be considered. Expert advice must be obtained. Meanwhile, if removal is imminent the port immigration authorities should be contacted immediately and it should be explained that proceedings are to be initiated. One should conclude by asking for removal to be delayed and (if appropriate) for temporary admission/release to be extended. A CIO will then consider the case and the request and phone back a short while later with a decision. Initially, removal will be delayed only for about a week; if proceedings are not under way by then, removal will take place.

If at all possible, the client's approval must be obtained before this delay procedure is used, and expert assistance must be enlisted at once.

5.7 Voluntary and supervised departure, expedited removal and alternative destinations

(a) Voluntary departure etc

(i) *Passengers at ports of entry* A passenger who has not been allowed to enter the UK may opt for immediate removal rather than commence or continue emergency proceedings. However, a disclaimer may have to be signed first (see appendix 1 group G).

(ii) *Prior to a decision to deport* Where no criminal proceedings are involved, a person may simply exit from the UK rather than risk being subject to a s3(5) decision to deport (see chapter 4.2). Where the person wishing to leave has been convicted of an offence, the procedure will differ depending on whether or not a deportation recommendation has been made. If there is no recommendation (and no decision to deport has been made), one may exit the country in the ordinary way (but see HC 169 paras 83 and 157 concerning prohibitions on re-entry). Where a recommendation has been made, see below.

(iii) *Once a decision to deport has been made* Persons recommended for deportation and persons facing a deportation order under s3(5)(c) (see chapter 4.2 para *(e)*) may agree voluntarily to depart to live "permanently" abroad (s5(6)). This course is not advised as it may exclude one from ever re-entering the UK. In any event, persons facing a s3(5)(c) order will be given an opportunity to depart voluntarily when told of their appeal right; they can depart *rather* than appeal, or *after* an appeal has been dismissed (HC 169 para 160). No provision refers to persons facing orders under s3(5)(a) and (b) (see chapter 4.2 para *(e)*). There is nothing to stop such persons from simply exiting the country. If they do so, the Home Office should be informed immediately so as to prevent the signing of a deportation order. An order made *after* one has simply exited the country will be revoked.

However, a person in respect of whom a decision to deport has been made may be in detention (Sch 3 para 2(2)). If such a person wishes to leave the UK as soon as possible (but is not eligible for official voluntary departure) removal may be expedited. Written notice waiving all appeal rights should be sent to the Home Office and a quick removal requested.

(iv) *Once a deportation order has been made* Persons whose whereabouts are not known to the Secretary of State and who possess valid travel documents can and do exit from the UK in the normal way. If detained, however, or if the authorities are holding the passport, then again one can only seek to expedite removal in pursuance of the order.

(v) *Alleged illegal entrants* When such a person has not yet been arrested then of course it is possible simply to exit the country. Once arrested and served with an IS 151 A (see 4.2 para (*h*)) one may opt for immediate departure rather than commence or continue emergency proceedings. However, a disclaimer may have to be signed first (see appendix 1 group G).

(b) Supervised departure etc

Supervised departure (with a prohibition on re-entry) is available paticularly in the case of young or first offenders who wish to leave the UK as soon as possible (HC 169 para 156). The Home Office is less likely to allow supervised departures in relation to other offenders.

If, having been refused supervised departure, the client still wishes to leave quickly, then, again, written notice waiving any appeal rights should be sent to the Home Office and the sentencing court should be contacted to ensure that the "certificate of recommendation" has been prepared and sent to the Deportation Machinery Group. Expedited removal can then be made.

(c) Alternative destinations

The destination specified in removal directions may be challenged on appeal in certain circumstances (see, especially, the appeals and time limits chart on pp38–39). If *no* such appeal exists, or if it has not been brought or was dismissed, it is still perfectly possible to arrange for removal to an alternative destination. The same requirements as apply to appeals will apply to special arrangements of this sort with the immigration authorities (see chapter 5.5 para *(c)*(ii) and HC 169 para 169).

Appendix 1

Forms

Contents

Group F: concerning immigration appeals

APP 201	(notice of appeal against entry clearance officer)
IS 87	(notice of appeal against immigration officer)
APP 1	(notice of appeal against Secretary of State)
APP 2	(application for leave to appeal from adjudicator to the Tribunal)

Group G: concerning detention and removal

IS 83 A	(notice to captain/detention on board)
IS 91	(detention order)
IS 101	(disclaimer/voluntary departure)

Appendix 1 group A: concerning passengers who may be—or who have been—refused entry

Five very common forms have been selected in this category. First comes the IS81, which requires the passenger to submit to further examination. This form will only be used *prior* to a decision on the passenger's application for leave to enter. If temporary admission is granted the IS96 (granting temporary admission) and the IS81 will usually be issued together. The day before having to report back to the immigration office one should *always* telephone to enquire whether the passenger's attendance is still required. Very often it is not, and the temporary admission will be extended over the telephone. The reference number on the IS81 or 96 should be noted: at this stage it will denote that no decision has yet been made (for example, "TN3/IS 81/. . .").

Once examination has been completed, a decision will invariably be made within 12 hours. If leave is granted, the official record will be the endorsement in the passport. However, an IS84 may cancel that leave. Only minor categories of entrants are issued with formal notices granting leave. These include aircrew (IS123) and persons arriving by yacht (IS18). Notice refusing leave to enter is given on IS82 or 82A, 82B or 82C. The plain 82 is for passengers with a right of appeal exercisable before removal. The 82C is the most common and is for passengers who may appeal only after leaving. The IS82 series incorporates removal directions and if removal is prevented (for example, by a stop order) then further directions may be given by an IS92. Note that once leave has been refused, the port preference will change to denote refusal (for example "TN3/RLE/. ."). The RLE stands for "refusal of leave to enter".

IS 81

Port Reference:
Home Office Reference:

HOME OFFICE
Immigration Service

HM IMMIGRATION OFFICE

Terminal No. 3, Heathrow Airport (London),
Hounslow, Middlesex TW6 1ND
Telephone:

IMMIGRATION ACT 1971 – NOTICE TO A PERSON REQUIRED TO SUBMIT TO FURTHER EXAMINATION

To . . . .

A. You have arrived at this port from . . . .
by ship/aircraft . . . . on . . . . 198 . . . .
and are a person to whom paragraph 2 of Schedule 2 to the Act applies.

B. You have been examined by an Immigration Officer* and you may also be required to be examined by a Medical Inspector**

C. **You are hereby required to submit to further examination by an Immigration Officer*****

Date Immigration Officer

* Paragraph 2(1) of Schedule 2 to the Act
** Paragraph 2(2) of Schedule 2 to the Act
*** Paragraph 2(3) of Schedule 2 to the Act

(IS 81 Further examination)

IS 82

HOME OFFICE
Immigration Service

Port Reference:
Home Office Reference:

HM IMMIGRATION OFFICE

Terminal No. 3, Heathrow Airport (London),
Hounslow, Middlesex TW6 1ND
Telephone:

IMMIGRATION ACT 1971 – NOTICE OF REFUSAL OF LEAVE TO ENTER

To

I therefore refuse you leave to enter the United Kingdom.

REMOVAL DIRECTIONS A. I have given/propose to give directions for your removal at . . . . hrs, on . . . . 198 . . . . by ship/aircraft . . . .
to (country/territory) . . . .

RIGHT OF APPEAL B. You are entitled * to appeal against refusal of leave to enter or against the decision that you require leave to enter; you are also entitled to appeal ** against removal/in appealing to object to being removed to the country or territory specified above. Any such appeal will be considered by the independent appellate authorities established for the purposes of the Act.

HOW TO APPEAL C. If you wish to appeal you should tell me or another immigration officer **before** the ship or aircraft leaves, or complete and return form IS 87 if you wish to give notice of appeal in writing.

If you decide to appeal after you have been removed, you should send written notice of appeal to me, addressed to HM Inspector at the above address, **to arrive not later than 28 days after your departure from the United Kingdom.**

ASSISTANCE AND ADVICE D. The United Kingdom Immigrants Advice Service (UKIAS) is a voluntary organisation independent of the Government. If you wish, they will advise you about the decision which has been taken against you and represent you at your appeal hearing. This assistance is confidential and free. Please ask if you wish to be put in touch with UKIAS.

You may also contact your High Commission or Consul or anyone else you think may be able to help you.

This notice has been explained to you in English . . . . by me/. . . . .

Date | Immigration Officer

* Section 13(1) of the Act
** Section 17 of the Act

(IS 82 RLE/Appeal before/after removal)

IS 84

HOME OFFICE
Immigration Service

Port Reference:
Home Office Reference:

HM IMMIGRATION OFFICE

Terminal No. 3, Heathrow Airport (London),
Hounslow, Middlesex TW6 1ND
Telephone:

IMMIGRATION ACT 1971 – NOTICE CANCELLING LEAVE TO ENTER

To

A. You have been examined by an Immigration Officer* and on .... 198 ...., you were given written notice of leave to enter the United Kingdom**

B. **I hereby cancel the notice of that leave to enter** and I am giving you a separate notice refusing you leave to enter the United Kingdom***

Date Immigration Officer

* paragraph 2(1) of schedule 2 to the Act.
** paragraph 6(1) of schedule 2 to the Act.
*** paragraph 6(2) of schedule 2 to the Act.

(IS 84 Cancellation within 12 hours)

HOME OFFICE
Immigration Service

Port Reference:
Home Office Reference:

IS 92

HM IMMIGRATION OFFICE

Terminal No. 3, Heathrow Airport (London),
Hounslow, Middlesex TW6 1ND
Telephone:

IMMIGRATION ACT 1971 – NOTICE OF FURTHER REMOVAL DIRECTIONS

To ....

• You were refused leave to enter the United Kingdom on ....
......198 ....

• I have now given directions for your removal from the United Kingdom*
by (ship/aircraft) ....to (country/territory)..........
at ......hrs, on ....198 ..

Date Immigration Officer

* Paragraph 8 of Schedule 2 to the Act

(IS 92 Further RD's after RLE)

IS 96

HOME OFFICE
Immigration Service

Port Reference:
Home Office Reference:

HM IMMIGRATION OFFICE

Terminal No. 3, Heathrow Airport (London),
Hounslow, Middlesex TW6 1ND
Telephone:

IMMIGRATION ACT 1971 – NOTIFICATION OF TEMPORARY ADMISSION TO A PERSON WHO IS LIABLE TO BE DETAINED

To ....

LIABILITY TO DETENTION A. You are a person who is liable to be detained*

TEMPORARY ADMISSION/ RESTRICTIONS B. I hereby authorise your (further) temporary admission to the United Kingdom subject to the following restrictions**:-

• You must reside at :- ....
....
....

• You must report to

Tick ☑ as appropriate

- ☐ an Immigration Officer } at ....
- ☐ the Police } ....
- ☐ on .... 198. . . . ., at . . . . hrs.
- ☐ each .... .day at .... .hrs until further notice.
- ☐ ....

ANY CHANGE OF RESTRICTION If these restrictions are to be changed, an Immigration Officer will write to you .

• **Although you have been temporarily admitted, you remain liable to be detained**
• **You have NOT been given leave to enter the United Kingdom within the meaning of the Immigration Act 1971**

Date **Immigration Officer**

* **Paragraph 16 of Schedule 2 to the Act**
** **Paragraph 21 of Schedule 2 to the Act.**

(IS 96 Temporary Admission)

Appendix 1 group B: concerning persons refused permission to stay longer in the UK

Whereas the forms in group A are issued by the Immigration Service, the group B forms are issued in the name of the Secretary of State in that *after* entry into the UK, decisions concerning extensions, variation and the like will be made by the Secretary of State (ie, by B1 Division at Lunar House in Croydon).

Three commonly used forms have been selected in this category. The first is the RON 110 which is used where the refused application was made *after* the applicant's previous limited leave had expired. Accordingly no right of appeal exists against the unfavourable decision.

The APP 101 and APP 103 are part of the series "APP 101–109" and the APP denotes a right of appeal. The 101 is very common indeed and is issued where the unfavourable decision is appealable. Variations of this notice are the 101A and 101 (EEC). The latter states that, although no right of *appeal* is available, the unsuccessful applicant may request an *extra-statutory review*. Since the recent Tribunal decision in *Lubbersen* [1984] 3 CMLR 77 the APP 101 (EEC) should be seen as wrong in law as that case decided that a statutory right of appeal *does* exist.

The Secretary of State is reviewing all the forms issued in his name and, no doubt, the 101(EEC) will be one of the forms abandoned or modified as a result of that review.

The APP 103 is issued when a person unsuccessfully applies for a certificate of entitlement (which certificate proves the holder has the right of abode in the UK and is therefore not subject to immigration control). The 103 explains that a right of appeal exists. Do not be surprised if the 103 is issued to a person whose previous limited leave expired before the unsuccessful application was made. This is not an indulgence by the Secretary of State but, in the authors' submission, indicative that the right of appeal does not depend on the applicant having had current leave when the application for a certificate was made.

Finally, note the Home Office reference number which should appear on the notice of refusal. This number will be the first letter of the applicant's surname followed usually by six digits.

RON 110

IMMIGRATION ACT 1971

Refusal to grant leave to remain or to vary leave to enter

To

The Secretary of State therefore refuses your application.

Under section 14(1) of the Immigration Act 1971 an entitlement to appeal against a refusal to vary a limited leave is conferred only on a person whose limited leave to enter or remain has not expired.

Your application was made on but your limited leave expired on You therefore have no right of appeal against the Secretary of State's decision.

I have to remind you that because your limited leave to enter or remain has expired you should leave the United Kingdom without delay. If you fail to leave you may be prosecuted for an offence under the Immigration Act, the penalty for which is a fine of up to £200 and up to six months' imprisonment, and you will also be liable to deportation.

Signed:

On behalf of the Secretary of State

Date:

Home Office
Immigration and Nationality Department

Form APP 101

IMMIGRATION ACT 1971

Refusal to revoke or vary leave to enter or remain

To

The Secretary of State therefore refuses your application.

You are entitled to appeal against this decision under section 14(1) of the Immigration Act 1971 to the independent appellate authorities established under that Act. If you wish to appeal you should complete the attached form and return it to the Under Secretary of State, Home Office (Appeals Section), Lunar House, Wellesley Road, CROYDON CR9 2BY, to arrive NOT LATER THAN 14 DAYS AFTER THE DATE OF THIS NOTICE. The Home Office will transmit your notice of appeal to the appellate authorities.

The United Kingdom Immigrants Advisory Service, a voluntary organisation independent of the Government, will advise you, if you wish, about the decision which has been taken against you and on whether to exercise your right of appeal. If you decide to appeal, the Service can also help you to prepare your appeal and to present it to the appellate authorities. These services are provided free of charge. The London office of the Service is at 7th Floor, Brettenham House, Savoy Street, Strand, London WC2E 7EP (telephone 01–240 5176). The Service has other offices at Birmingham, Folkestone, Leeds, Manchester, Southampton, Heathrow Airport, Gatwick Airport and Glasgow.

Signed:
On behalf of the Secretary of State

Date:

Home Office
Immigration and Nationality Department

IMMIGRATION ACT 1971
Refusal of certificate of entitlement to right of abode

To

The Secretary of State therefore refuses your application.

You are entitled to appeal against this decision under section 13(2) of the Immigration Act 1971 to the independent appellate authorities established by that Act. If you wish to appeal you should complete the attached notice of appeal and return it to the Under Secretary of State, Home Office (Appeals Section), Lunar House, Wellesley Road, CROYDON, CR9 2BY to arrive *not later than 14 days* after the date of this notice. The Home Office will transmit your notice of appeal to the appellate authorities.

The United Kingdom Immigrants Advisory Service, a voluntary organisation independent of the Government, will advise you, if you wish, about the decision which has been taken against you and on whether to exercise your right of appeal. If you decide to appeal, The Service can also help you to prepare your appeal and to present it to the appellate authorities. These services are provided free of charge. The London office of the Service is at 7th Floor, Brettenham House, Savoy Street, Strand, London, WC2E 7EP (telephone 01-240-5176). The Service also has offices at Birmingham, Folkestone, Leeds, Manchester, Southampton, Heathrow Airport, Gatwick Airport and Glasgow.

Signed:
On behalf of the Secretary of State

Date:

Home Office
Immigration and Nationality Department

Appendix 1 group C: concerning persons being deported

Whereas the forms shown in group B are generally issued by the part of the Home Office responsible for general casework (B1 Division), the forms concerning deportation are generally issued by B3 Division.

In this category, two forms from the "APP 101–109" series have been selected as well as an example of a deportation order.

The APP 104 gives notice that a deport decision has been taken pursuant to the Immigration Act s3(5). The 104 is never issued in respect of decisions taken pursuant to s3(6) (ie as the result of a court recommendation) in that s3(6) decisions are not appealable and so there is no legal duty under the Immigration Appeals (Notices) Regulations to give formal notice of such a decision. So the very fact that a 104 has been issued is indicative of the fact that no court recommendation has been made. However, note that the 104 (like any formal notice) is not required by the Notice Regulations to be issued where the whereabouts of the person concerned are not known to the Home Office. Accordingly, in appropriate cases one should ask B3 Division whether or not notice of a deport decision has been served "on file".

Where a person does not appeal against a deport decision, or where that appeal fails, then a deportation order will normally be signed and removal directions will be given. The APP 107 will then be issued. As it clearly states, at this stage the actual deportation order cannot be challenged through the immigration appeal system. There may be little or no merit in the destination appeal offered by the 107, but in a particular case it may be essential to bring the appeal in order to buy time.

IMMIGRATION ACT 1971
Decision to make a deportation order

To

The Secretary of State has therefore decided to make an order by virtue of section 3(5) of the Immigration Act 1971 requiring you to leave the United Kingdom and prohibiting you from entering while the order is in force. He proposes to give directions for your removal to

You are entitled to appeal against this decision under section 15(1)(a) of the Act to the independent appellate authorities established under the Act, and under section 16(3) of the Act you are entitled in appealing to object to the country specified above. If you wish to appeal you must complete the attached form and return it to the Under Secretary of State, Home Office (Appeals Section), Lunar House, Wellesley Road, CROYDON CR9 2BY, to arrive *not later than 14 days after the date of this notice.* The Home Office will transmit your notice of appeal to the appellate authorities. If you wish to be removed to a country not specified above it will be for you to satisfy the appellate authorities that the government of the country of your choice would admit you on deportation from the United Kingdom, and you should be prepared to produce evidence to that effect.

The United Kingdom Immigrants Advisory Service, a voluntary organisation independent of the Government, will advise you, if you wish, about the decision which has been taken against you and on whether to exercise your right of appeal. If you decide to appeal, the Service can also help you to prepareyour appeal and to present it to the appellate authorities. These services are provided free of charge. The London Office of the Service is at 7th Floor, Brettenham House, Savoy Street, Strand, London WC2E 7EP (telephone 01-240-5176). The Service also has offices at Birmingham, Folkestone, Leeds, Manchester, Southampton, Heathrow Airport, Gatwick Airport and Glasgow.

Signed:
On behalf of the Secretary of State

Date:

Home Office
Immigration and Nationality Department

IMMIGRATION ACT 1971
Deportation Order

Whereas

not being patrial within the meaning of the Immigration Act 1971, and having only limited leave to enter the United Kingdom, has remained beyond the time limited by the leave and is, accordingly, liable to deportation by virtue of section 3(5)(a) of the said Act:

Now, therefore, in pursuance of section 5(1) of the said Act, I by this order require the said

to leave and prohibit from entering the United Kingdom so long as this order is in force.

And in pursuance of paragraph 2(3) of Schedule 3 to the said Act, I hereby authorise to be detained until is removed from the United Kingdom.

One of Her Majesty's Principal
Secretaries of State

Home Office
Queen Anne's Gate

IMMIGRATION ACT 1971
Directions for removal on deportation

To

The Secretary of State has made a deportation order against you in pursuance of section 5(1) of the Immigration Act 1971, and has given directions for your removal from the United Kingdom on or as soon as possible thereafter by to

You have no appeal against deportation, but you are entitled to appeal against the removal directions under section 17(1)(b) of the Immigration Act 1971 to the dependent appellate authorities established under the Act, on the ground that you ought not to be removed to the country specified in the directions, but ought to be removed to some other country or territory specified by you.

If you wish to appeal on that ground you should complete the enclosed form and return it to the Under Secretary of State, Home Office (Appeals Section), Lunar House, Wellesley Road, Croydon CR9 2BY, to arrive NOT LATER THAN 14 DAYS AFTER THE DATE OF THIS NOTICE. The Home Office will transmit your notice of appeal to the appellate authorities. You should attach to the form a statement of the reasons why you object to removal to the country specified in the directions. It is for you to satisfy the appellate authorities that the government of the country of your choice would admit you on deportation from the United Kingdom, and you should be prepared to produce evidence to that effect.

The United Kingdom Immigrants Advisory Service, a voluntary organisation independent of the Government, will advise you, if you wish, about the decision which has been taken against you and on whether to exercise your right of appeal. If you decide to appeal the Service can also help you to prepare your appeal and to present it to the appellate authorities. These services are provided free of charge. The London Office of the Service is at 7th Floor, Brettenham House, Savoy Street, Strand, London WC2E 7EP (telephone 01-240-5176). The Service also has offices at Birmingham, Folkestone, Leeds, Manchester, Southampton, Heathrow Airport, Gatwick Airport and Glasgow.

Signed:
On behalf of the Secretary of State

Date:

Home Office
Immigration and Nationality Department

Appendix 1 group D: concerning persons being treated as illegal entrants

Handling illegal entry cases is the responsibility of the Immigration Service. This means the IO or CIO in the local Immigration Service office. One's first approach, therefore, should always be to the IO or CIO in the case. It is that officer who, when satisfied that the suspicion of illegal entry has been established, will issue the IS 151 A. The form tells the recipient that s/he is considered to be an illegal entrant and that removal directions will follow separately.

The appeals and the time limits chart on pp38–39, above, explains that, generally, an illegal entrant may only appeal the validity of removal directions and that appeal may only be brought after removal. Such persons will be issued with an IS 151 D. On the other hand, a person whose entry was illegal in that it was in defiance of a current deportation order may additionally appeal the destination to which it is intended s/he should be removed. That appeal may be brought before removal and such persons will be issued with an IS 151 E.

It should be noted that, although the principal point of contact in illegal entry cases is the IO or CIO at the appropriate Immigration Service office, every illegal entry case must be filtered through the Illegal Entry Unit at the Service's headquarters in Lunar House, Croydon. Removal cannot take place until the unit's authorisation has been obtained. The unit also conducts a monthly review of all illegal entrants in detention (with a view to granting temporary release).

It is often useful to ask the IO or CIO whether or not a particular case has yet passed through the Illegal Entry Unit and, occasionally, it is necessary to telephone the unit in connection with a case.

There are, of course other forms with which illegal entrants may be issued, but the IS 151 A, D and E have been selected because they are commonly used and well illustrate the operation of appeal rights.

IS 151A

HOME OFFICE
Immigration Service

Port Reference:
Home Office Reference:

HM IMMIGRATION OFFICE

IMMIGRATION ACT 1971 – NOTICE TO AN ILLEGAL ENTRANT

To ....

I have considered all the information available to me and I am satisfied that you are an illegal entrant as defined in section 33(1) of the Immigration Act 1971.

LIABILITY TO DETENTION A. You are therefore a person who is liable to be detained pending the completion of arrangements for dealing with you under the Act.* I propose to give directions for your removal from the United Kingdom in due course and details will be given to you separately.

DETENTION/ TEMPORARY ADMISSION B. I hereby authorise

☐ your detention in ....
(please see the notice below).

☐ your temporary admission in the United Kingdom**. The conditions attached to this are explained on the form IS 96 which is enclosed.

Tick ☑ *as appropriate*

Date Immigration Officer

* Paragraph 16 of Schedule 2 to the Act
** Paragraph 21 of Schedule 2 to the Act

Important notice for persons detained under the Immigration Act 1971. You may wish to draw the information below to the attention of your legal adviser. It explains your legal position and your right to make contact while in custody.

Section 62 of the Criminal Law Act 1977 states: "Where any person has been arrested and is being held in custody in a police station or other premises, he shall be entitled to have intimation of his arrest and of the place where he is being held, sent to one person reasonably named by him without delay or, where some delay is necessary in the interest of the investigation or the prevention of crime or the apprehension of offenders, with no more delay than is so necessary."

If you are not satisfied that your entitlement as quoted above has been made clear to you, please tell the officer named above.

(IS 151A, Illegal Entrant)

IS 151D

HOME OFFICE
Immigration Service

Port Reference:
Home Office Reference:

HM IMMIGRATION OFFICE

IMMIGRATION ACT 1971 – NOTICE OF REMOVAL TO AN ILLEGAL ENTRANT

To ....

On .... 198. . . . .you were served with notice, IS 151A, that you are an illegal entrant as defined in section 33(1) of the Immigration Act 1971.

REMOVAL DIRECTIONS A. Direction have now been given for your removal from the United Kingdom* by (ship/aircraft) .... to (country/territory) .... at ....hrs on .... 198 .....

RIGHT OF APPEAL B. You are entitled to appeal to the independent appellate authorities against these directions on the ground that the facts of the case are such that there is in law no power to give the directions. You may appeal only **after** you have left the United Kingdom**.

HOW TO APPEAL C. If you wish to appeal, you should complete the enclosed form IS 87 and send it to HM Inspector at the address above. **It must arrive not later than 28 days after your departure from the United Kingdom.** I will then send the form to the appellate authorities.

ASSISTANCE AND ADVICE D. The United Kingdom Immigrants Advisory Service (UKIAS) is a voluntary organisation, independent of the Government. If you wish they will advise you about this decision and represent you at your appeal hearing. This service is confidential and free.
You may also contact your High Commission or Consul or anyone else you think may be able to help you.

The contents of this notice have been explained to you in English/ .... by me/ ....

Date

Immigration Officer

* Paragraph 9 or 10 of Schedule 2 to the Act
** Section 16(1) of the Act

(IS 151D Removal of Illegal entrant/appeal after removal)

IS 151E

HOME OFFICE
Immigration Service

Port Reference:
Home Office Reference:

HM IMMIGRATION OFFICE

IMMIGRATION ACT 1971 – NOTICE OF REMOVAL TO A PERSON WHO IS SUBJECT TO A CURRENT DEPORTATION ORDER

To ....

On .... 198 ...., you were served with notice, IS 151A, that you are an illegal entrant as defined in section 33(1) of the Immigration Act 1971.

REMOVAL DIRECTIONS A. Directions have now been given for your removal from the United Kingdom* by (ship/aircraft) .... to (country/territory) .... at .... hrs on .... 198 ....

RIGHT OF APPEAL B. You are entitled to appeal to the independent appellate authorities against these directions on the following grounds

- **Before** removal, that you ought to be removed (if at all) to a different country or territory named by you**
- **Before or after** removal, that you are not the person named in the deportation order***
- **After** removal, that there is no power in law to give the directions****

HOW TO APPEAL C. If you wish to appeal **before** removal, you should

- tell me or another Immigration Officer **before** the departure of the ship/aircraft in which you are to be removed from the United Kingdom or,
- complete the enclosed form, IS 87, which should be received by HM Inspector at the above address before your departure and **not later than 14 days after the date of this notice**

If you wish to appeal **after** removal from the United Kingdom you should complete the enclosed form IS 87, and return it to HM Inspector at the above address. It must arrive **not later than 28 days after your departure from the United Kingdom.** I will then send the form to the appellate authorities.

ADVICE AND ASSISTANCE D. The United Kingdom Immigrants Advisory Service (UKIAS) is a voluntary organisation, independent of the Government. They will advise you, if you wish, about the decision which has been taken against you, and represent you at your appeal hearing. This service is confidential and free.

You may also contact your High Commission or Consul or anyone else you think may be able to help you.

The contents of this notice have been explained to you in English/ .... by me/ ....

Date

Immigration Officer

* paragraph 9 or 10 of Schedule 2 to the Act
** section 17(1)(c) of the Act
*** section 16(2) of the Act
**** section 16(1) of the Act

(IS 151E Removal of deportee/appeal before removal)

Appendix 1 group E: concerning the making of representations

The letter, below, from David Waddington MP (Minister responsible for immigration) to MPs and Lords indicates the present practice regarding representations. The following item is an example of a typical representation. Note the technique and emotive style.

MINISTER OF STATE

HOME OFFICE
QUEEN ANNE'S GATE
LONDON SW1H 9AT

14 JUL 1983

Dear Colleague,

You will of course know that as the Minister responsible for Immigration a great deal of my time is taken up looking into representations about cases by Members of both Houses. This is as it should be, but I am concerned at the way in which the system is now working. One of the problems is that as a result of successive rounds of representations, perhaps by a number of different Members, people with no real claim to be here can spin out their stays. What is more important, individuals can suffer as a result of being detained for long periods or left in a prolonged state of anxiety about their future. Considering all these representations in detail also results in frustrating delays for the many deserving applicants whose cases are not taken up by Members.

I am sure therefore you will agree that we need to have more sensible arrangements for handling representations; and I am equally sure that the cornerstone of these arrangements must be the constituency MP. What I intend to do therefore is this. In future I will consider in detail the first representations I receive, from which ever House they come. However, if it is apparent that these do not come from the constituency Member but the constituency Member can be readily identified, I will notify that Member of the fact that representations have been made and give him or her the opportunity to comment if he or she wishes to do so. I think it is reasonable to say that generally speaking stays on decisions taken after the first representations - and any comments from the constituency MP in a case taken up by someone else - have been considered will not be made unless there are significant new facts. I recognise that this cannot be an inflexible rule; but on the other hand it cannot, I feel, be right to allow cases to be prolonged indefinitely by repeated re-examination of previous arguments.

I do assure Members that I have no intention of operating these guidelines inflexibly and will do all I can to help when approached about a case. But I do believe that by adopting this basic procedure a fairer system for all concerned will develop and there will be a useful improvement in the handling of these difficult matters.

Yours Sincerely
David Waddington
(DAVID WADDINGTON)

TOWER HAMLETS LAW CENTRE

341 Commercial Road,
London E1 2PS

Tel. 01-791 0741

Your ref:

My ref:

Secretary of State for the Home Department,
50 Queen Anne's Gate,
London SW1

Dear Sir,

[name]

I have been instructed by the above person, a citizen of
On at Stansted Airport he was refused leave to enter on the ground of an outstanding deportation order. This representation is to request the Secretary of State to exercise his discretion exceptionally by revoking the outstanding deportation order against Mr and regularise his status in the UK with an exceptional grant of leave to enter.

Mr was born in on . Prior to his first entry to the UK he was employed as a telephone technician in . He was single. He first entered the UK in July 1974 with the vague intention of investigating the academic possibilities here. He was eager to realise his potential, and as an intelligent man he wished to do so through further study. He was granted leave to enter as a visitor.

He investigated academic possibilities and registered for a three-year degree course at College of Technology in electrical engineering in 1974. He successfully completed this course in 1977.

The beginning of this course of studies marks the start of Mr 's immigration problems in that he did not apply for variation of leave to remain as a student prior to the expiry of his leave. I state most strongly that this failure was not motivated by any contempt for the law; instead he was obsessively fearful that permission would be refused and that he would be unable to study in the UK. Had Mr sought legal advice at that point, he would have been informed that his application was sound. This is the irony of the situation.

He embarked upon a three-year degree programme at a recognised institution which required full-time, daytime course of study and for which Mr
paid his own tuition fees and accommodation and maintenance costs. Funds for

this purpose were remitted to him from . Mr did not work during this time. Further, I must emphasise that at this time Mr 's clear intention was to return to at the completion of his period of study in the UK. Documentation substantiating these facts is either enclosed or will be forwarded under separate cover. Accordingly, it is clear that he had, prima facie, a sound application for variation of leave.

During his degree course he met his present wife . They were married on 30.4.77 (marriage certificate enclosed). was born in on and first entered the UK on at the age of nine and has been settled here ever since. 's nationality status is not certain. She is probably a citizen of (not a British citizen) but at the very least she has been settled here since 1967 and has an entitlement to citizenship by registration (BNA 1981 s7(1)(a)).

We would point out that *had* Mr obtained leave to remain as a student then at the time of his marriage he would have been a commonwealth citizen with leave to remain in a temporary capacity. Accordingly, in the light of the above, at the time of his marriage Mr would have fallen within the provisions of paras 26 and 26A of HC 239 which came into effect on 22.3.77. Under those provisions he would have been able to apply for 12 months followed by settlement on the basis of his marriage to a settled spouse. Again the irony of the situation is apparent: prima facie he had a perfectly sound application to make as a student — but he did not — had he done, he would have had a perfectly valid application to make for 12 months followed by settlement. I would urge the Secretary of State to distinguish between someone who would never have fallen within the rules at a specific time and someone who given legal advice would, prima facie, have fallen squarely within the provisions in force at the time.

Accordingly it is clear that, without altering any of the facts of the case, Mr , had he had the benefit of simple legal advice, would have been settled here ever since 1978. I urge the Secretary of State to take this into account and put it to Mr 's credit.

In the summer of 1977 twins were born to the couple (birth certificates enclosed). The fifth member of the family unit is a son born to before she met . The natural father of this child is unknown and there is no contact between him and and the child. Instead, Mr has accepted full responsibility for the child and considers himself the child's father. All the children are attending school and it is a happy and stable family. The family have remained at the same address for over five years and the children continue to attend the same school.

After the successful completion of his degree course, Mr enrolled as a part time student at the Polytechnic of in a two-year course in electrical and electronic engineering as Mr wished to improve his qualifications.

Now, for the first time since he entered the UK Mr took employment on a part time basis to support his family. His only other alternative would have been to claim social security which he did not wish to do and indeed has never done. At the successful completion of this course of studies Mr was offered a post in his field by City University. The University regarded him highly and gave him day release and sponsored him for a further two year diploma course at the Polytechnic of Central London in electronic and computer technology. In total, Mr studied for seven years. From 1981 he was employed full time by City University. (Letter of recommendation enclosed.)

In September 1982 Mr received a telegram from informing him that his father had suffered a stroke. He sought and was granted a leave of absence from City University and went to . Once there, he realised that he could not be certain how long it would take his father to recover and decided that the only honourable course of action was to resign his post at City University which he did. He also became ill himself briefly. Though eager to be reunited with his family, in early 1983 he was required by law to serve a one year non-military form of national service for graduates. He was desolate at being apart from his wife and children. In December 1983–1984 he used his period of leave to return to the UK on a visit to be with his family. He is firm that the immigration officer at the port of entry was informed of the true nature of his visit and his circumstances.

Once discharged from the national service in early 1984, Mr had to attend to various family matters, then returned to the UK in September 1984. He was refused leave to enter on the basis of the outstanding deportation order against him. This was the first time Mr knew anything about a deportation order. If Mr had received notice of the intention of the Secretary of State to make a deportation order, then Mr 's position might still have been saved through an appeal. Regrettably though, he failed to receive that notice.

These, then are the circumstances of Mr 's case and I would argue that there are strong grounds for reviewing his case with compassion.

Firstly, as I have already indicated he has been a victim of ignorance rather than a person who could never have been brought within the law. He has used his decade in the UK to gain an education and expertise for which his last employer regarded him highly. He is a devoted family man with two young children and one step-son all born in the UK and all attending school here. Neither his wife nor any of his children has ever been to . If Mr is forced to return to then it would cause extreme hardship to the rest of his family. They could not manage without his emotional and financial support, yet if they accompanied him they would be forced into a culture of which they know nothing and confronted by a language alien to them. Were the children infants they might have adapted, but this is not the case. Further, , 26, is still very close to her own family who live close by and with whom she has regular contact. and and the children are religious people and members of their local church. They are highly regarded as members of their congregation. (Letter from Father David is enclosed, from the Bishop of Stepney to follow under separate cover.)

Bearing in mind that: the family unit is so well established and rooted in the UK; that Mr has been and if permitted will continue to be an upstanding member of his community; that his family would suffer extreme hardship if forced to follow him to ; that equally they would suffer without his support and be forced to resort to social security; and that the deportation order against him was signed in ignorance of his circumstances rather than as a consequence of them, I would urge in the strongest possible terms the Secretary of State to review and investigate this case and acknowledge the exceptional nature of it.

On behalf of   I apply for an exceptional revocation of the deportation order and exceptional grant of leave to enter for an indefinite period.

I would be happy to assist in any way I can.

Yours faithfully,

Appendix 1 group F: concerning immigration appeals

Where an entry clearance officer (abroad), an IO (at a port of entry) or the Secretary of State (at the Home Office in Croydon) makes an appealable decision, when notice of that decision is given, a blank "notice of appeal" form will also be issued. To bring a first instance appeal (ie an appeal against the decision of the immigration authority) one must either complete the blank "notice of appeal" form or write a letter providing the same details as are required by the form. The completed form, or letter, must then be returned to the immigration authority which took the decision that is being appealed.

The blank notice of appeal form is based on "Form 1" in the Schedule to the old Immigration Appeals (Procedure) Rules of 1972. Under those old Rules, completing and returning the blank form was the only method by which notice of appeal could be given. The entry clearance officers' version of the "Form 1" is the APP 201; the IO version is the IS 87 and the Secretary of State's version is the APP 1. The old Procedure Rules were in force until 1 March 1985. Although the current Rules make no mention of blank notice of appeal forms and although "Form 1" has been erased from the Schedule, the APP 201, IS 87 and APP 1 will continue to be issued and may still be used to give notice of appeal as before.

Photocopied forms may be used, so one is advised to maintain a copied supply. Very often, notice of appeal must be given without delay yet for one reason or another the blank form that was issued may not be available.

It is emphasised that particular attention must be given to the question of simultaneous destination appeals. That is to say, where a destination appeal is to be brought in the context, for example, of a deportation appeal, on the notice of appeal one must state the objections to the specified destination and indicate the evidence which tends to show that admission to an alternative territory will be possible.

Where the adjudicator dismisses an appeal, application may be made for leave to appeal to the Tribunal. Whereas there are three different notice of appeal forms, there is only one "application for leave to appeal" form. This is the APP 2. Again, it originates from the Schedule to the old Procedure Rules and, again, it is still being issued and is in use despite the fact that the current Rules make no reference to it.

Both sides of each of the four forms discussed above are shown on the following pages.

Form APP 201

IMMIGRATION ACT 1971

Notice of appeal to an adjudicator

To the Adjudicator

Particulars of Appellant

Full names: (Forenames) (Surname)
(Block letters)

Date of birth:

Nationality/Citizenship:

Address:

Particulars of decision appealed against

A copy of the notice of the decision or action appealed against is annexed hereto.

The grounds of appeal are as follows:-

Please turn over

Full name and address of appellant's representative in the United Kingdom, if any, (see Note 2 below).

Signed ....
(Appellant or authorised representative)

Date ....

Notes: 1. **This form with any supporting documents you wish to provide will be sent by the entry clearance officer to an adjudicator in the United Kingdom for consideration of your appeal. You will be informed of his decision in due course. Any original documents you send will be returned to you.**

2. **You may if you wish ask a relative, friend, solicitor, voluntary organisation or other person in the United Kingdom to act as your representative. He will be given an opportunity to appear before the adjudicator and/or to submit evidence to him in writing.**

Immigration
Appeals
(Procedure)
Rules 1972

Form 1

H.O. Form I.S. 87

IMMIGRATION ACT 1971

<u>Notice of appeal to adjudicator</u>

To the Adjudicator

The appellant is -

giving notice of appeal/*and applying for bail (<u>see Note (a) overleaf</u>)

<u>Particulars of Appellant</u>

Full name: (Forenames) (Surname)
(Block letters)

Date of birth:

Nationality/Citizenship:

Address:

(<u>If detained give address where detained</u>)

Particulars of decision or action appealed against:-

A copy of the notice of the decision or action appealed against is annexed hereto.

The grounds of appeal are as follows/*attached

---

* The appellant objects to removal to the country/territory to which he is to be removed, namely on the grounds set out in the attached statement (<u>see Note (b) overleaf</u>).

A hearing of the appeal *is/*is not requested (<u>see Note (c) overleaf</u>).

Address to which this form should be sent:	Signed .... (Appellant or authorised Representative) Date ....

Immigration
Appeals
(Procedure)
Rules 1972
Form 1

* Delete words which are inapplicable

Notes

(a) An application for bail should normally be supported by the appropriate form, which will be given to you on application but may be made orally.

Such an application may be made after notice of appeal has been given.

(b) An objection to removal to a particular country or territory must be accompanied by a written statement giving the grounds for the objection.

(c) Where an appellate authority disposes of an appeal without a hearing the case is considered on the basis of the written submissions made by the respective parties to the appeal.

(d) If a hearing is requested and you are to be represented please give details of your representative.

Name

Address

Form APP 1

IMMIGRATION ACT 1971

Notice of appeal to an adjudicator or Tribunal at first instance

Delete words which are inapplicable

To the Adjudicator/Tribunal

The appellant is - giving notice of appeal
applying for bail (see note (a) overleaf)

Particulars of Appellant

Full names: (Block letters) (Forenames) (Surname)

Date of birth:

Nationality/Citizenship

Address
(If detained
give address
where detained)

Particulars of decision or action appealed against:-

A copy of the notice of the decision or action appealed against is annexed hereto.

The grounds of appeal are as follows:-

The appellant objects to removal to the country/territory to which he is to be removed, namely   on the grounds set out in the attached statement (see Note (b) below).

Delete words which are inapplicable

A hearing of the appeal is/is not requested (see Note (c) below)

Immigration Appeals (Procedure) Rules 1972

Signed.....................................
(Appellant or authorised representative)

Date ....

Notes

(a) An application for bail should normally be supported by the appropriate form, but may be made orally.
Such an application may be made after notice of appeal has been given.

(b) An objection to removal to a particular country or territory must be accompanied by a written statement giving the grounds for the objection.

(c) Where an appellate authority disposes of an appeal without a hearing the case is considered on the basis of the written submissions made by the respective parties to the appeal.

Form APP 2

IMMIGRATION ACT 1971

Notice of appeal or application for leave to appeal from adjudicator

To the *Adjudicator/*Tribunal

The appellant is - *applying for leave to appeal to the Tribunal
*giving notice of appeal to the Tribunal
*applying for bail (see Note (a) overleaf)

Particulars of Appellant

Full names: (Forenames) (Surname)
(Block letters)

Date of birth:

Nationality/Citizenship

Address:

(If detained give address where detained)

Particulars of determination of the adjudicator appealed against:-

---

A copy of the notice of the determination of the adjudicator appealed against is annexed hereto.

The grounds of appeal are as follows:-

---

*The appellant wishes to adduce further evidence before the Tribunal as follows:-

* Delete words which are inapplicable

*The appellant objects to removal to the country/territory to which he is to be removed, namely
on the grounds set out in the attached statement (see Note (b) below)

A hearing of the appeal *is/*is not requested

Signed ....

(Appellant or authorised representative)

Date ....

---

*Delete words which are inapplicable

*Endorsement

Leave to appeal has been *granted/*refused

Signed ....

(Adjudicator/President/Chairman of the Tribunal)

Immigration Appeals (Procedure) Rules 1972

Form 2

Notes

(a) An application for bail should normally be supported by the appropriate form, but may be made orally. Such an application can be made subsequently.

(b) An objection to removal to a particular country or territory must be accompanied by a written statement as to the reasons for the objection.

Appendix 1 group G: concerning detention and removal

There is a wide variety of forms concerning detention and removal—some are for issue to the person who is to be detained or removed, while others are for issue to airlines, prison authorities and the like. Only three forms have been selected, though: the IS 83A and 91, both of which concern detention, and the IS 101 which relates to voluntary departure with a disclaimer.

The IS 83A is of particular interest because it is rarely seen by practitioners (it is issued only to the captain of a ship or aircraft) yet it relates to questions often asked by persons who are to be deported or otherwise removed. These questions include "Will I be like any other passenger on the ship/plane?" and "Will I be free to disembark before my final destination?". The IS 83A shows that UK law enables the Immigration Service to require a captain to ensure that removal directions are fulfulled. For this purpose, the captain may even resort to detaining the passenger. It is probably the case that the 83A finds a very mixed reception among captains of non-British shipping and airlines. Accordingly, where the Immigration Service feels that such is warranted, a passenger may be given a police escort all the way to the final destination. Whether or not there is to be an escort and, if so, whether it is to be a police officer or some other person, is to a limited extent open to negotiation, in the authors' experience.

The IS 91 is the basic order to detain and is addressed to the police, prison service, or Securicor. It is complemented by the IS 150 A (not shown here) which orders the detention of illegal entrants and crewmembers. The IS 91 is modified in different circumstances; the 91A orders the detention under the Immigration Act of a person who is in any event a remand prisoner in a criminal matter, while the 91B orders immigration detention in respect of a person who is in any event a convicted prisoner serving a sentence.

Finally, the IS 101 is used very often where a detainee decides to agree to removal rather than to commence or to continue representations, appeals and the like. It is submitted that there is nothing in law to prevent a person from withdrawing or revoking a signed disclaimer prior to removal.

Apart from the forms discussed above, it should be noted that some of the forms displayed in other groups within this appendix also make provision for detention and removal.

IS 83A

Port Reference:
Home Office Reference:

HOME OFFICE
Immigration Service

HM IMMIGRATION OFFICE

Terminal No. 3, Heathrow Airport (London), Hounslow, Middlesex TW6 1ND
Telephone:

IMMIGRATION ACT 1971 – NOTICE TO CAPTAIN TO DETAIN PERSON(S) ON BOARD HIS SHIP OR AIRCRAFT

To the Captain of (ship/aircraft) ....

Name(s) ....

....

....

A. I have directed that the person(s) named above be placed on board your ship/aircraft* and I have directed that he/she/they be removed from the United Kingdom** by (ship/aircraft) .... to (country/territory) .... at .... hrs on .... 198 ....

B. I require you to prevent the person(s) named above from disembarking

- in the United Kingdom or
- before the directions for his/her/their removal have been fulfilled,

and for this purpose you may detain the person(s) named above in custody on board***

Date Immigration Officer

* paragraph 11 or 15 of Schedule 2 to the Act
** paragraph 8(1)(c), 10, 12(2)(c), 13(2)(c) or 14 of Schedule 2 to the Act
*** paragraph 16(4) of Schedule 2 to the Act

(IS 83A Notice to Captain/detention on board)

IS 91

HOME OFFICE
Immigration Service

Port Reference:
Home Office Reference:

HM IMMIGRATION OFFICE

Terminal No. 3, Heathrow Airport (London),
Hounslow, Middlesex TW6 1ND
Telephone:

IMMIGRATION ACT 1971 – AUTHORITY FOR DETENTION

To *Tick [✓] as appropriate*

☐ the Commissioner of Police for the Metropolis
☐ the Chief Constable of . . . .
☐ the Governor, HM Prison/Remand Centre . . . .
☐ Securicor Ltd. . . . .

Name. . . . .

Date of birth . . . . .Nationality . . . .

AUTHORITY FOR DETENTION A. Please receive the person named above, whose detention I have authorised*

COSTS B. In this case
☐ the cost of detention and any escort should be charged to Messrs . . . .
. . . .(see note below)
☐ the cost will be defrayed by the Secretary of State.

Date Immigration Officer

* Paragraph 16 of Schedule 2 to the Act.

NOTE – to be completed by the Immigration Officer when costs are to be charged to the carrier.

Any invoice to the carrying company should contain these details;
- port reference number as at the top of this letter.
- persons arrival details: at (place) . . . . .on . . . . .198 . . . . . .
from . . . . .by (ship/aircraft) . . . .

(IS 91 Detention order)

IS 101

HOME OFFICE
Immigration Service

Port Reference:
Home Office Reference:

HM IMMIGRATION OFFICE

Terminal No. 3, Heathrow Airport (London),
Hounslow, Middlesex TW6 1ND
Telephone:

IMMIGRATION ACT 1971 – DISCLAIMER IN THE CASE OF VOLUNTARY DEPARTURE

To the Immigration Officer

A. I, ...

understand that ....(person or group) is/are

making representations on my behalf.

B. Nevertheless I wish to return to ....(country) as soon as possible

Tick ☑ *as appropriate*

- ☐ at my own expense
- ☐ at the expense of the carrying company
- ☐ at the expense of the Secretary of State

without waiting for the outcome of those representations.

Signed ....

The person named above signed this statement in my presence.

Signed ....

Full name (CAPITALS) ....

Date ....

Time ....

Place ....

(IS 101 Disclaimer/voluntary departure)

Ac

FOREIGN AND COMMONWEALTH OFFICE **(01) 213-3000**
Phone for addresses, phone numbers, telex numbers etc. of British High Commissions and Embassies around the world.

IMMIGRATIO
NATIONALIT

Lunar House,
Croydon, Surre

B1 **B2** **B3 DIVISION** **B4**

Responsible for enforcement other than that which is carried out by the Immigration Service; ie B3 is responsible for DEPORTATION.

THE DEPORTATION MACHINERY GROUP (DMG)
'Lunar House'
EXT: 2722

B3 will also play a part in Immigration Service cases if representations are made through an MP or if judicial review proceedings are commenced. B3 has connections with the Ministers' private offices (see top right) and with Treasury Solicitor.

TREASURY SOLICITOR (01) 233-6975

Within B3, three deportation casework groups divide the work according to the LAST TWO DIGITS OF THE HOME OFFICE REFERENCE NUMBER:

	Phone 'Lunar House'
Casework Group 3 S...ref nos. 01-34	EXT: 2633
Casework Group 3 V...ref nos. 35-67	EXT: 2543
Casework Group 3 X...ref nos. 68-00	EXT: 2555

Where no reference number is known, simply 'phone the Deportation Machinery Group, above.

THE APPEALS SECTION

The DMG instructs the po
detained deportees. The pc
case are:

LONDON: ALIENS REG
DEPORT SEC
(01) 725-2196/

ELSEWHERE: THE ALI
AT ALL F

B3 provides the presenting officers (POs) for hearings Thanet House.
HOME OFFICE
POs UNIT
AFRICA HOUSE
64-78, KINGSWAY,
LONDON, WC2
(01) 405-2716

THANET HOUSE
231 STRAND,
LONDON, WC2
(01) 353-8060

POLICY

CUSTODY AND DETENTION

SHORT TERM

HARMONDSWORTH DETENTION CENTRE (near Heathrow)
(01) 897-2302 (switchboard)
(01) 897-8040 (Securicor)
(01) 759-1849 (to speak to detainees)

HEATHROW:
Queen's Building Detention Centre
(01) 759-9280 and 9372

Port cases and, at Harmondsworth, illegal entry cases. Both centres run by SECURICOR on a Home Office contact

GATWICK: (0293) 30731/24284

BIRMINGHAM: (021) 743-2813

DOVER: (0304) 206260 (East docks)
(0304) 203203 ext. 3308 (West docks)

FOLKESTONE: (0303) 54202

HARWICH: (02555) 2141

LONG TERM

HARMONDSWORTH DETENTION CENTRE (see left for details)
ASHFORD REMAND CENTRE, MIDDLESEX. The Deport Block is used (men only) for persons detained under the Immigration Act. Phone Ashford 41041

HOLLOWAY PRISON (REMAND WING), LONDON. Women detainees only. Phone (01) 607-6747

NB: PERSONS MAY ALSO BE DETAINED IN THE REMAND WING OF PRISONS OR, BRIEFLY, IN POLICE STATIONS. WHEN PHONING THE FORMER, DIRECT ENQUIRIES TO "RECEPTION" OR "THE DISCIPLINE OFFICE". IF IN DOUBT, CONTACT "THE PRISONS DEPT", ECCLESTON SQUARE, LONDON SW1—(01) 828-9848

HE
Insp
Insp
Imm
Insp
and
The

GA
CIO
Hea

INT
an I
enfo

ISIS
was
It st
com
of B
is re
side

tem

When making contact, always have the client's completed questionnaire nearby.

HOME OFFICE

Public switchboards:
(01) 686-0688 (immigration)
(01) 681-3241 (nationality)

Internal Lunar House switchboard:
(01) 686-0333 and ask for the extension you require.

Ministers' Private Offices
50, Queen Anne's Gate, London SW
(01) 213-3000
Phone to request temporary stop order if MP unobtainable

HOUSE OF COMMONS/LORDS
Phone **(01) 219-3000** and ask for the MP/Peer by name. If the MP's name is not known, ask for the Library and state the constituency.

B5

E (ARO)

I SECTION
STATIONS

IMMIGRATION SERVICE

Primarily responsible for port of entry cases and enforcement against illegal entrants. Most of the former are dealt with entirely at the port. However, every illegal entrant case must be filtered through HQ. For such cases, phone 'Lunar House' **EXT: 2570**

ntres the Home
Immigration office

DSWORTH:
41 (hearing)
9 (POs)

ntres:
HAM:
382

26
STER:
571
IPTON:
0

Headquarters at Lunar House, Croydon
H.M. CHIEF INSPECTOR

DEPUTY CHIEF INSP. (enforcement—the Illegal Entry Unit)

DEPUTY CHIEF INSP. (Heathrow & airports)

DEPUTY CHIEF INSP. (administration)

A number of Assistant Chief Inspectors

When phoning any Immigration Service office, ask for 'CASEWORK' (CIO Level)

NT

NDON AREA

1 & 2 share an Assistant Chief
s its own. Each Terminal also has
tion Officers (CIOs) and
. The Assistant Chief Inspector and
y and cover 8.00 am–10.00pm. CIOs
day, every day.
TERMINAL 1: (01) 759-7715/6
TERMINAL 2: (01) 897-3129
TERMINAL 3: (01) 897-9631

Chief Inspector, various Inspectors,
are on duty same hours as at
8822 for the Immigration Office.

HARMONDSWORTH: Headed by
sponsible for investigation and
de of London. Phone **(01) 897-0771**

ARK: Headed by an Inspector, this
ation Office for the Port of London.
' cases (eg. private pleasure craft
also conducts interviews on behalf
learance officers but, principally, it
tion and enforcement on the east
) 928-6824.

REST OF UK

The Assistant Chief Inspectorate is structured on an areas basis (eg. the South East). Individual offices will therefore usually be staffed by Inspectors, CIOs and IOs.

BELFAST: (0232) 22547
(08494) 52500 (weekends)
* **BIRMINGHAM: (021) 743-4272**
BRISTOL: (027587) 2843
CARDIFF: (0222) 396127
* **DOVER: (0304) 204192** (East docks)
(0304) 201913 (West docks)
(0304) 207513 (Hoverport)
EDINBURGH: (031) 344-3330
* **FOLKESTONE: (0303) 56541**
GLASGOW: (041) 887-4115
GRAVESEND: (0474) 52308
* **HARWICH: (02555) 4371**
HULL: (0482) 223017

LEEDS: (0532) 603126
LIVERPOOL: (051) 236-8974
LUTON: (0582) 421891
MANCHESTER RINGWAY: (061) 437-2402
NEWCASTLE: (0632) 869469
PRESTWICK: (029) 78675
RAMSGATE: (0843) 54716
SHEERNESS: (07956) 67733
SOUTHAMPTON: (07032) 29027

* The asterisk denotes a separate phone number for the port's detention centre–see the bottom left of the chart.

Appendix 2

Access to the Immigration Authorities: Offices and Organisations

When dealing with an emergency the appropriate immigration authority will have to be contacted in order, firstly, to determine or confirm the facts of the case and, secondly, to make requests (for example, for temporary admission).

The various authorities and their telephone numbers are contained within the chart on the following pages. That chart is a modification of the one appearing on pp8–9, and its purpose is to give the necessary details in the context of the structure of immigration control.

It is impossible to state with precision whom one should telephone first—much depends on the nature of the case and how much information is known. The following may be useful, though:

(a) trouble at port on arrival—contact the port Immigration Service office;
(b) if detained at a police station, ask: "under whose authority?"
    (i) if the police—ask for the officer in the case
    (ii) if on the basis of an outstanding deportation order—contact the Aliens Registration Office (deport section) or B3 division;
    (iii) if the Immigration Service—contact the Service's local office.

The following points should be noted:

(a) concerning illegal entry cases, all of them without exception must be "filtered" through the Illegal Entry Unit at Immigration Service Headquarters. This unit is responsible to a deputy chief inspector and in no case can a final decision be made without the involvement and consent of the Unit. An illegal entry case can also find its way to B3 if an MP has intervened or if one has moved for judicial review.

    As a general rule in illegal entry cases, first contact the local Immigration Service office and ask if the case has yet gone up to HQ and, if so, whether removal directions have yet been authorised;
(b) concerning port of entry cases, these very seldom go higher than CIO level. Regarding temporary admission, it is very unusual for HQ to overturn the decision taken at the port. However, whenever an asylum application is made, the case will always be referred upwards (as the Immigration Rules say the "Home Office" must then take the decision); and

(c) concerning deportation, one should always enquire whether or not an order has been made "on file" (the Notice Regulations reg 3(4) states that where a person's whereabouts are not known the decision need not be notified).

Other useful organisations are listed on p111.

Organisations which advise and assist to varying degrees

Citizens Advice Bureaux
(see local telephone directory or contact the National Association—NACABS—on 01-833 2181)

Community Relations Councils
(see local telephone directory or contact the Commission for Racial Equality on 01-828 7022)

Immigration Law Practitioners' Association (ILPA)
115 Old Street
London EC1V 9JR
Tel: 01-250 1671

Joint Council for the Welfare of Immigrants (JCWI)
115 Old Street
London EC1V 9JR
Tel: 01-251 8706

Law centres
(see local telephone directory or contact the Law Centres Federation on 01-387 8570)

United Kingdom Immigrants Advisory Service (UKIAS)
7th Floor
Brettenham House
Savoy Street
Strand
London WC2
Tel: 01-240 5176

Asylum

British Refugee Council
Bondway House
3–9 Bondway
London SW8
Tel: 01-582 6922

UKIAS Refugee Unit
8th Floor
Brettenham House
Savoy Street
Strand
London WC2
Tel: 01-397 7969

World University Service
20–21 Compton Terrace
London N1
Tel: 01-226 6747
(for educational rights)

Employment

Department of Employment
(Overseas Labour Section)
Caxton House
Tothill Street
London SW1
Tel: 01-213 6055

Students

National Union of Students
1 Endsleigh Street
London WC1
Tel: 01-387 1277

United Kingdom Council for Overseas Student Affairs (UKCOSA)
60 Westbourne Grove
London W2
Tel: 01-229 9268

Welfare

British Refugee Council (above)
(welfare advice for refugees)

Child Povery Action Group (CPAG)
1 Macklin Street
London WC2
Tel: 01-242 3225

DHSS (Overseas Branch)
Longbenton
Newcastle-upon-Tyne NE98 1YX
Tel: 0632-793356

Voluntary repatriation

International Social Service of Great Britain (ISS)
Cranmer House
39 Brixton Road
London SW9
Tel: 01-735 8941

Readers' own addresses and telephone numbers

Appendix 3

Bibliography and Further Reading

Please note that this appendix is not a comprehensive guide to reading materials on immigration and nationality—it is simply a selection made by the authors.

Source materials

Immigration Act 1971
The governing statute, which came into force on 1 January 1973. See appendix 6.

Immigration Rules (HC 169)
The current set of Rules, which came into force on 16 February 1983. The Rules have been amended three times, see p7.

Immigration Appeals (Procedure) Rules 1984 SI No 2041
These Rules came into force on 1 March 1985 and relate, inter alia, to the bringing of appeals.

The above items can be purchased from Her Majesty's Stationery Office (HMSO). Readers are strongly advised to obtain a copy of the Immigration Rules. The Immigration Act itself is not really a good buy in that it cannot be relied upon in its unamended form. The Act, as amended, is therefore reproduced in appendix 6.

General immigration and nationality

British Nationality: the AGIN Guide to the New Law by Ian Martin with Ann Dummet, NCCL 1982
This book deals only with nationality and is extremely enlightening and compact. Very inexpensive, it should be seen as an essential purchase for anyone with a working knowledge of nationality.

British Nationality Law and the 1981 Act by Laurie Fransman, Fourmat 1982
Again, this book deals only with nationality. It is about to be expanded in a second edition. It is clearly written and illustrated with charts. Newcomers to nationality have found it very helpful.

Immigration Law and Practice by Lawrence Grant and Ian Martin, Cobden Trust 1982
This book is regarded as the straightforward general practitioner's text on immigration and nationality. Still in its first edition, the law is good only up to 30 June 1981, but a 1985 supplement has updated it to June 1984.

Immigration Law and Practice by Ian Macdonald, Butterworths 1983
Like Grant and Martin (above) Macdonald deals with both immigration and nationality. The law is good up to 12 February 1983, thus it refers both to the new Nationality Act and to the current Immigration Rules (HC 169). It is an advanced practitioner's book and, on the whole, is probably too rarified for persons dealing with the odd application or emergency.

In addition, information sheets, pamphlets and booklets on various aspects of immigration and nationality law and practice are published by the organisations listed below. Readers are advised to write to each requesting a list of current publications.

Joint Council for the Welfare of Immigrants (JCWI)
115 Old Street
London EC1

Action Group on Immigration and Nationality (AGIN)
c/o 115 Old Street
London EC1

The Runnymede Trust
178 North Gower Street
London NW1

Further, there are two principal subscription services:

JCWI Bulletin
Approximately six issues a year. Write to JCWI at the above address for subscription details.

Immigration Law–Bulletin of the Immigration Law Practitioners' Association
Published quarterly through the Frank Cass publishing house. Write to ILPA, 115 Old Street, London EC1V 9JR.

Appeals

Tribunals Practice and Procedure John Bowers (general editor); Laurie Fransman (immigration author), Legal Studies and Services and Hemstal Press, 1985

See also Grant and Martin, op cit, chapter 14 and Macdonald, op cit, chapter 11.

Campaigns

For an example of a campaign kit which itself contains excellent general advice, see "*Immigration Widows" Kit*, available from Women, Immigration and Nationality Group (WING) c/o 115 Old Street, London EC1.

Detention

See the series of papers (particularly no 4) entitled *Immigration Prisoners Project* published jointly by JCWI (see above for address) and the Prison Reform Trust, Nuffield Lodge, Regents Park, London NW1 4RS.

Judicial review

Judicial Review by Kenneth Bagnall QC, Profex 1985

See also the *Notes for Guidance* issued by the Crown Office (which are reproduced in Bagnall, op cit, above).

Passports: how to interpret endorsements

See Grant and Martin, op cit, appendix 2.

Larry Grant "Remaining in the United Kingdom 1 Examining the Passport" July 1979 *LAG Bulletin* 155 and also Sue Gray and Anthea Lowe *The Ins and Outs of Immigration and Nationality Law*, NACAB 1983, pp25–33.

Welfare benefits and immigration

Immigrants and the Welfare State by Wendy Collins and Hugo Storey, NACAB 1983.

Appendix 4

Client Questionnaire

A Personal details

1. Client's name. (If more than one name note them all but distinguish the name(s) which are written in his or her travel document.)
2. Date of birth.
3. Address and telephone number.
4. Nationality. (If more than one, all should be noted.)
5. Marital status.
6. Details of present or previous spouse(s). (Including names, nationality, and date of marriage.)
7. Details of parents. (Including their names, place of birth, and nationality.)
8. Details of grandparents. (In particular, their nationality.)
9. Present whereabouts of spouse/parents. (If they are in the UK their immigration status should be noted.)
10. Children. (Names, dates of birth, nationality and whereabouts.)
11. If the "contact person" is not the client, their name, address, telephone number and relationship to the client should be noted.
12. Whether the client speaks sufficient English or if an interpreter in a particular language is required.

B Immigration history

Entries

1. Date of first entry into the UK, and the purpose of entry.
2. Date of any subsequent arrivals/departures and their purpose of entry.
3. The purpose for which leave to enter/remain is currently being sought. (One must clearly establish the client's wishes.)

Passport

1. Government that issued the client's passport.
2. Date of expiry of passport.
3. If a British passport, is the holder described as a British Dependent Territories citizen, a British Overseas citizen etc.

C The emergency

1 The reason legal advice is sought. What does the client/contact believe is the problem?
2 Which forms/letters have recently been issued to the client by the authorities?

Emergencies at the port of entry

1 Flight details (including the airport the passenger was travelling from) and the date and time of arrival.
2 The reference number used by the Immigration Service.
3 Whether or not passenger obtained entry clearance before travelling.
4 Has a decision to refuse entry been made? If so, when was this and what reasons were given? If no decision has yet been reached enquire as to what matters are causing concern, and whether a further interview of the passenger has been arranged or is anticipated.
5 Have removal directions been given, and if so, the date, time, and flight number relating to the planned removal.
6 Whether the person has been released (for example, on temporary admission or bail) or is in detention. (If on temporary admission, any "conditions" should be noted. If in detention, see below.)
7 The name of any MP/Peer already involved and the nature/extent of his or her involvement.

Emergencies concerning people already present in the UK

1 Relevant details and date(s) of decisions made by the authorities. (For example, the date a notice of intention to deport was signed or the client was sentenced by a court.)
2 The reference number used by the Immigration Service/Home Office.
3 Whether a right of appeal existed/exists and/or representations have been made.
4 Whether the client has been released (for example, on temporary admission or bail) or is in detention. (Any "conditions" attached to the release should be noted. If in detention, see below.)

If in detention

1 Place of detention.
2 Address and telephone number. (Also see appendix 2.)
3 Details required to obtain bail or temporary release for example, whether the person has a fixed address, stable family background etc.

Appendix 5

Visa Requirements

NATIONALS OF FOREIGN COUNTRIES WHO NEED VISAS FOR THE UNITED KINGDOM

Europe

Nationals of Albania, Bulgaria, Czechoslovakia, German Democratic Republic, Hungary, Poland, Romania, USSR.

Asia

Nationals of Pakistan who seek admission to the United Kingdom in accordance with paragraphs 31, 32, 35, 38, 39, 40–42 and 46–55 of this statement and nationals of all other countries except Bahrain, Israel, Japan, Kuwait, Republic of Korea, Qatar, Turkey and United Arab Emirates.

Africa

Nationals of all countries except Algeria, Ivory Coast, Morocco, Niger, Tunisia and the Republic of South Africa.

America

Nationals of Cuba and the Argentine Republic.

CITIZENS OF COMMONWEALTH COUNTRIES WHO NEED VISAS FOR THE UNITED KINGDOM

Citizens of Sri Lanka (other than those to whom paragraph 77(*a*) applies).

[*The above information is set out in the Appendix to HC 169 as amended by Cmnd 9539.*]

Appendix 6

The Immigration Act 1971 as amended

Since coming into force on 1 January 1973 the Immigration Act 1971 has been amended by a number of statutes ranging from the Criminal Justice Act 1972 to the Police and Criminal Evidence Act 1984. The most important amendments were brought about by the British Nationality Act 1981.

Below is reproduced the 1971 Act *as amended*. However, Schs 4–6, which for present purposes are unimportant, have been omitted.

An Act to amend and replace the present immigration laws, to make certain related changes in the citizenship law and enable help to be given to those wishing to return abroad, and for purposes connected therewith.

[28th October 1971]

PART I

REGULATION OF ENTRY INTO AND STAY IN UNITED KINGDOM

General principles

1.—(1) All those who are in this Act expressed to have the right of abode in the United Kingdom shall be free to live in, and to come and go into and from, the United Kingdom without let or hindrance except such as may be required under and in accordance with this Act to enable their right to be established or as may be otherwise lawfully imposed on any person.

(2) Those not having that right may live, work and settle in the United Kingdom by permission and subject to such regulation and control of their entry into, stay in and departure from the United Kingdom as is imposed by this Act; and indefinite leave to enter or remain in the United Kingdom shall, by virtue of this provision, be treated as having been given under this Act to those in the United Kingdom at its coming into force, if they are then settled there (and not exempt under this Act from the provisions relating to leave to enter or remain).

(3) Arrival in and departure from the United Kingdom on a local journey from or to any of the Islands (that is to say, the Channel Islands and Isle of Man) or the Republic of Ireland shall not be subject to control under this Act, nor shall a person require leave to enter the United Kingdom on so arriving, except in so far as any of those places is for any purpose excluded from this subsection under the powers conferred by this Act; and in this Act the United Kingdom and those places, or such of them as are not so excluded, are collectively referred to as "the common travel area":

(4) The rules laid down by the Secretary of State as to the practice to be followed in the administration of this Act for regulating the entry into and stay in the United Kingdom of persons not having the right of abode shall include provision for admitting (in such cases and subject to such restrictions as may be provided by the rules, and subject or not to conditions as to length of stay or otherwise) persons coming for the purpose of taking employment, or for purposes of study, or as visitors, or as dependants of persons lawfully in or entering the United Kingdom.

(5) The rules shall be so framed that Commonwealth citizens settled in the United Kingdom at the coming into force of this Act and their wives and children are not, by virtue of anything in the rules, any less free to come into and go from the United Kingdom than if this Act had not been passed.

2.—(1) A person is under this Act to have the right of abode in the United Kingdom if—

(a) he is a British citizen; or

(b) he is a Commonwealth citizen who—

   (i) immediately before the commencement of the British Nationality Act 1981 was a Commonwealth citizen having the right of abode in the United Kingdom by virtue of section 2(1)(d) or section 2(2) of this Act as then in force; and

   (ii) has not ceased to be a Commonwealth citizen in the meanwhile.

(2) In relation to Commonwealth citizens who have the right of abode in the United Kingdom by virtue of subsection (1)(b) above, this Act, except this section and sections 3(9) and (9A), 5(2) and 13(3), shall apply as if they were British citizens; and in this Act (except as aforesaid) "British citizen" shall be construed accordingly.

[*Note:* s2 as in force prior to 1 January 1983 read as follows:

2.—(1) A person is under this Act to have the right of abode in the United Kingdom if—

Statement of right of abode, and related amendments as to citizenship by registration.

(a) he is a citizen of the United Kingdom and Colonies who has that citizenship by his birth, adoption, naturalisation or (except as mentioned below) registration in the United Kingdom or in any of the Islands; or

(b) he is a citizen of the United Kingdom and Colonies born to or legally adopted by a parent who had that citizenship at the time of the birth or adoption, and the parent either—

(i) then had that citizenship by his birth, adoption, naturalisation or (except as mentioned below) registration in the United Kingdom or in any of the Islands: or

(ii) had been born to or legally adopted by a parent who at the time of that birth or adoption so had it; or

(c) he is a citizen of the United Kingdom and Colonies who has at any time been settled in the United Kingdom and Islands and had at that time (and while such a citizen) been ordinarily resident there for the last five years or more; or

(d) he is a Commonwealth citizen born to or legally adopted by a parent who at the time of the birth or adoption had citizenship of the United Kingdom and Colonies by his birth in the United Kingdom or in any of the Islands.

(2) A woman is under this Act also to have the right of abode in the United Kingdom if she is a Commonwealth citizen and either—

(a) is the wife of any such citizen of the United Kingdom and Colonies as is mentioned in subsection (1)(a), (b) or (c) above or any such Commonwealth citizen as is mentioned in subsection (1)(d); or

(b) has at any time been the wife—

(i) of a person then being such a citizen of the United Kingdom and Colonies or Commonwealth citizen; or

(ii) of a British subject who but for his death would on the date of commencement of the British Nationality Act 1948 have been such a citizen of the United Kingdom and Colonies as is mentioned in subsection (1)(a) or (b);

but in subsection (1)(a) and (b) above references to registration as a citizen of the United Kingdom and Colonies shall not, in the case of a woman, include registration after the passing of this Act under or by virtue of section 6(2) (wives) of the British Nationality Act 1948 unless she is so registered by virtue of her marriage to a citizen of the United Kingdom and Colonies before the passing of this Act.

(3) In relation to the parent of a child born after the parent's death, reference in subsection (1) above to the time of the child's birth shall be replaced by references to the time of the parent's death; and for purposes of that subsection—

(a) "parent" includes the mother of an illegitimate child; and
(b) references to birth in the United Kingdom shall include birth on a ship or aircraft registered in the United Kingdom, or on an unregistered ship or aircraft of the Government of the United Kingdom, and similarly with references to birth in any of the Islands; and
(c) references to citizenship of the United Kingdom and Colonies shall, in relation to a time before the year 1949, be construed as references to British nationality and, in relation to British nationality and to a time before the 31st March 1922, "the United Kingdom" shall mean Great Britain and Ireland; and
(d) subject to section 8(5) below, references to a person being settled in the United Kingdom and Islands are references to his being ordinarily resident there without being subject under the immigration laws to any restriction on the period for which he may remain.

(4) In subsection (1) above, any reference to registration in the United Kingdom shall extend also to registration under arrangements made by virtue of section 8(2) of the British Nationality Act 1948 (registration in independent Commonwealth country by United Kingdom High Commissioner), but, in the case of a registration by virtue of section 7 (children) of that Act, only if the registration was effected before the passing of this Act.

(5) The law with respect to registration as a citizen of the United Kingdom and Colonies shall be modified as provided by Schedule 1 to this Act.

(6) In the following provisions of this Act the word "patrial" is used of persons having the right of abode in the United Kingdom.]

General provisions for regulation and control.

3.—(1) Except as otherwise provided by or under this Act, where a person is not a British citizen—

(a) he shall not enter the United Kingdom unless given leave to do so in accordance with this Act;
(b) he may be given leave to enter the United Kingdom (or, when already there, leave to remain in the United Kingdom) either for a limited or for an indefinite period;
(c) if he is given a limited leave to enter or remain in the United Kingdom, it may be given subject to conditions restricting his employment or occupation in the United Kingdom, or

requiring him to register with the police, or both.

(2) The Secretary of State shall from time to time (and as soon as may be) lay before Parliament statements of the rules, or of any changes in the rules, laid down by him as to the practice to be followed in the administration of this Act for regulating the entry into and stay in the United Kingdom of persons required by this Act to have leave to enter, including any rules as to the period for which leave is to be given and the conditions to be attached in different circumstances; and section 1(4) above shall not be taken to require uniform provision to be made by the rules as regards admission of persons for a purpose or in a capacity specified in section 1(4) (and in particular, for this as well as other purposes of this Act, account may be taken of citizenship or nationality).

If a statement laid before either House of Parliament under this subsection is disapproved by a resolution of that House passed within the period of forty days beginning with the date of laying (and exclusive of any period during which Parliament is dissolved or prorogued or during which both Houses are adjourned for more than four days), then the Secretary of State shall as soon as may be make such changes or further changes in the rules as appear to him to be required in the circumstances, so that the statement of those changes be laid before Parliament at latest by the end of the period of forty days beginning with the date of the resolution (but exclusive as aforesaid).

(3) In the case of a limited leave to enter or remain in the United Kingdom—

(a) a person's leave may be varied, whether by restricting, enlarging or removing the limit on its duration, or by adding, varying or revoking conditions, but if the limit on its duration is removed, any conditions attached to the leave shall cease to apply; and

(b) the limitation on and any conditions attached to a person's leave may be imposed (whether originally or on a variation) so that they will, if not superseded, apply also to any subsequent leave he may obtain after an absence from the United Kingdom within the period limited for the duration of the earlier leave.

(4) A person's leave to enter or remain in the United Kingdom shall lapse on his going to a country or territory outside the common travel area (whether or not he lands there), unless within the period for which he had leave he returns to the United Kingdom in circumstances in which he is not required to obtain leave to enter; but, if he does so return, his previous leave (and any limitation on it or conditions attached to it) shall continue to apply.

(5) A person who is not a British citizen shall be liable to

deportation from the United Kingdom—

(a) if, having only a limited leave to enter or remain, he does not observe a condition attached to the leave or remains beyond the time limited by the leave; or

(b) if the Secretary of State deems his deportation to be conducive to the public good; or

(c) if another person to whose family he belongs is or has been ordered to be deported.

(6) Without prejudice to the operation of subsection (5) above, a person who is not a British citizen shall also be liable to deportation form the United Kingdom if, after he has attained the age of seventeen, he is convicted of an offence for which he is punishable with imprisonment and on his conviction is recommended for deportation by a court empowered by this Act to do so.

(7) Where it appears to Her Majesty proper so to do by reason of restrictions or conditions imposed on British citizens, British Dependent Territories citizens or British Overseas citizens when leaving or seeking to leave any country or the territory subject to the government of any country. Her Majesty may by Order in Council make provision for prohibiting persons who are nationals or citizens of that country and are not British citizens from embarking in the United Kingdom, or from doing so elsewhere than at a port of exit, or for imposing restrictions or conditions on them when embarking or about to embark in the United Kingdom; and Her Majesty may also make provision by Order in Council to enable those who are not British citizens to be, in such cases as may be prescribed by the Order, prohibited in the interests of safety from so embarking on a ship or aircraft specified or indicated in the prohibition.

Any Order in Council under this subsection shall be subject to annulment in pursuance of a resolution of either House of Parliament.

(8) When any question arises under this Act whether or not a person is a British citizen, or is entitled to any exemption under this Act, it shall lie on the person asserting it to prove that he is.

(9) A person within this subsection seeking to enter the United Kingdom and claiming to have the right of abode there shall prove that he has that right by means of such certificate of entitlement as may be specified in the immigration rules, unless—

(a) he claims to be a British citizen and produces (or is present when there is produced) a United Kingdom passport describing him as such a citizen or a United Kingdom passport describing him as a citizen of the United Kingdom and Colonies having the right of abode in the United Kingdom; or

(b) in the case of a woman falling within subsection (9A)(b) below who claims to be a British citizen as there mentioned by virtue of section 2(2) of this Act as in force immediately before the commencement of the British Nationality Act 1981, she shows that immediately before that commencement she—

(i) was a citizen of the United Kingdom and Colonies; and

(ii) had the right of abode in the United Kingdom by virtue of section 2(2) of this Act, as then in force, apart from any reference therein to section 2(1)(c) or (d) as then in force.

(9A) A person is within subsection (9) above if—

(a) he is not a British citizen; or

(b) he claims to be a British citizen by virtue of section 11(1) of the British Nationality Act 1981 on the ground that immediately before the commencement of that Act he had the right of abode in the United Kingdom by virtue of section 2(1)(c) or section 2(2) of this Act, as then in force.

Administration of control.

4.—(1) The power under this Act to give or refuse leave to enter the United Kingdom shall be exercised by immigration officers and the power to give leave to remain in the United Kingdom, or to vary any leave under section 3(3)(a) (whether as regards duration or conditions), shall be exercised by the Secretary of State; and, unless otherwise allowed by this Act, those powers shall be exercised by notice in writing given to the person affected, except that the powers under section 3(3)(a) may be exercised generally in respect of any class of person by order made by statutory instrument.

(2) The provisions of Schedule 2 to this Act shall have effect with respect to—

(a) the appointment and powers of immigration officers and medical inspectors for purposes of this Act;

(b) the examination of persons arriving in or leaving the United Kingdom by ship or aircraft, and the special powers exercisable in the case of those who arrive as, or with a view to becoming, members of the crews of ships and aircraft; and

(c) the exercise by immigration officers of their powers in relation to entry into the United Kingdom, and the removal from the United Kingdom of persons refused leave to enter or entering or remaining unlawfully; and

(d) the detention of persons pending examination or pending removal from the United Kingdom;

and for other purposes supplementary to the foregoing provisions of this Act.

(3) The Secretary of State may by regulations made by statutory instrument, which shall be subject to annulment in pursuance of a resolution of either House of Parliament, make provision as to the effect of a condition under this Act requiring a person to register with the police; and the regulations may include provision—

(a) as to the officers of police by whom registers are to be maintained, and as to the form and content of the registers;

(b) as to the place and manner in which anyone is to register and as to the documents and information to be furnished by him, whether on registration or on any change of circumstances;

(c) as to the issue of certificates of registration and as to the payment of fees for certificates of registration;

and the regulations may require anyone who is for the time being subject to such a condition to produce a certificate of registration to such persons and in such circumstances as may be prescribed by the regulations.

(4) The Secretary of State may by order made by statutory instrument, which shall be subject to annulment in pursuance of a resolution of either House of Parliament, make such provision as appears to him to be expedient in connection with this Act for records to be made and kept of persons staying at hotels and other premises where lodging or sleeping accommodation is provided, and for persons (whether British citizens or not) who stay at any such premises to supply the necessary information.

Procedure for, and further provisions as to, deportation.

5.—(1) Where a person is under section 3(5) or (6) above liable to deportation, then subject to the following provisions of this Act the Secretary of State may make a deportation order against him, that is to say an order requiring him to leave and prohibiting him from entering the United Kingdom; and a deportation order against a person shall invalidate any leave to enter or remain in the United Kingdom given him before the order is made or while it is in force.

(2) A deportation order against a person may at any time be revoked by a further order of the Secretary of State, and shall cease to have effect if he becomes a British citizen.

(3) A deportation order shall not be made against a person as belonging to the family of another person if more than eight weeks have elapsed since the other person left the United Kingdom after the making of the deportation order against him; and a deportation order made against a person on that ground

shall cease to have effect if he ceases to belong to the family of the other person, or if the deportation order made against the other person ceases to have effect.

(4) For purposes of deportation the following shall be those who are regarded as belonging to another person's family—

(a) where that other person is a man, his wife and his or her children under the age of eighteen; and

(b) where that other person is a woman, her children under the age of eighteen;

and for purposes of this subsection an adopted child, whether legally adopted or not, may be treated as the child of the adopter and, if legally adopted, shall be regarded as the child only of the adopter; an illegitimate child (subject to the foregoing rule as to adoptions) shall be regarded as the child of the mother, and "wife" includes each of two or more wives.

(5) The provisions of Schedule 3 to this Act shall have effect with respect to the removal from the United Kingdom of persons against whom deportation orders are in force and with respect to the detention or control of persons in connection with deportation.

(6) Where a person is liable to deportation under section 3(5)(c) or (6) above but, without a deportation order being made against him, leaves the United Kingdom to live permanently abroad, the Secretary of State may make payments of such amounts as he may determine to meet that person's expenses in so leaving the United Kingdom, including travelling expenses for members of his family or household.

Recommendations by court for deportation.

6—(1) Where under section 3(6) above a person convicted of an offence is liable to deportation on the recommendation of a court, he may be recommended for deportation by any court having power to sentence him for the offence unless the court commits him to be sentenced or further dealt with for that offence by another court.

Provided that in Scotland the power to recommend a person for deportation shall be exercisable only by the sheriff or the High Court of Justiciary, and shall not be exercisable by the latter on an appeal unless the appeal is against a conviction on indictment or against a sentence upon such a conviction.

(2) A court shall not recommend a person for deportation unless he has been given not less than seven days notice in writing stating that a person is not liable to deportation if he is a British citizen describing the persons who are British citizens and stating (so far as material) the effect of section 3(8) above and section 7 below; but the powers of adjournment conferred by section 10(3) of the Magistrates' Courts Act 1980, section 179 or 380 of the

Criminal Procedure (Scotland) Act 1975 or any corresponding enactment for the time being in force in Northern Ireland shall include power to adjourn, after convicting an offender, for the purpose of enabling a notice to be given to him under this subsection or, if a notice was so given to him less than seven days previously, for the purpose of enabling the necessary seven days to elapse.

(3) For purposes of section 3(6) above—

(a) a person shall be deemed to have attained the age of seventeen at the time of his conviction if, on consideration of any available evidence, he appears to have done so to the court making or considering a recommendation for deportation; and

(b) the question whether an offence is one for which a person is punishable with imprisonment shall be determined without regard to any enactment restricting the imprisonment of young offenders or persons who have not previously been sentenced to imprisonment;

and for purpose of deportation a person who on being charged with an offence is found to have committed it shall, notwithstanding any enactment to the contrary and notwithstanding that the court does not proceed to conviction, be regarded as a person convicted of the offence, and references to conviction shall be construed accordingly.

(4) Notwithstanding any rule of practice restricting the matters which ought to be taken into account in dealing with an offender who is sentenced to imprisonment, a recommendation for deportation may be made in respect of an offender who is sentenced to imprisonment for life.

(5) Where a court recommends or purports to recommend a person for deportation, the validity of the recommendation shall not be called in question except on an appeal against the recommendation or against the conviction on which it is made; but the recommendation shall be treated as a sentence for the purpose of any enactment providing an appeal against sentence.

(6) A deportation order shall not be made on the recommendation of a court so long as an appeal or further appeal is pending against the recommendation or against the conviction on which it was made; and for this purpose an appeal or further appeal shall be treated as pending (where one is competent but has not been brought) until the expiration of the time for bringing that appeal or, in Scotland, until the expiration of twenty-eight days from the date of the recommendation.

(7) For the purpose of giving effect to any of the provisions of this section in its application to Scotland, the High Court of Justiciary shall have power to make rules by act of adjournal.

Exemptions from deportation for certain existing residents.

7.—(1) Notwithstanding anything in section 3(5) or (6) above but subject to the provisions of this section, a Commonwealth citizen or citizen of the Republic of Ireland who was such a citizen at the coming into force of this Act and was then ordinarily resident in the United Kingdom—

(a) shall not be liable to deportation under section 3(5)(b) if at the time of the Secretary of State's decision he had at all times since the coming into force of this Act been ordinarily resident in the United Kingdom and Islands; and

(b) shall not be liable to deportation under section 3(5)(a), (b) or (c) if at the time of the Secretary of State's decision he had for the last five years been ordinarily resident in the United Kingdom and Islands; and

(c) shall not on conviction of an offence be recommended for deportation under section 3(6) if at the time of the conviction he had for the last five years been ordinarily resident in the United Kingdom and Islands.

(2) A person who has at any time become ordinarily resident in the United Kingdom or in any of the Islands shall not be treated for the purposes of this section as having ceased to be so by reason only of his having remained there in breach of the immigration laws.

(3) The "last five years" before the material time under subsection (1)(b) or (c) above is to be taken as a period amounting in total to five years exclusive of any time during which the person claiming exemption under this section was undergoing imprisonment or detention by virtue of a sentence passed for an offence on a conviction in the United Kingdom and Islands, and the period for which he was imprisoned or detained by virtue of the sentence amounted to six months or more.

(4) For purposes of subsection (3) above—

(a) "sentence" includes any order made on conviction of an offence; and

(b) two or more sentences for consecutive (or partly consecutive) terms shall be treated as a single sentence; and

(c) a person shall be deemed to be detained by virtue of a sentence—

  (i) at any time when he is liable to imprisonment or detention by virtue of the sentence, but is unlawfully at large; and

  (ii) (unless the sentence is passed after the material time) during any period of custody by which under any relevant enactment the term to be served under the sentence is reduced.

In paragraph (c)(ii) above "relevant enactment" means section 67 of the Criminal Justice Act 1967 (or, before that section operated, section 17(2) of the Criminal Justice Administration Act 1962) and any similar enactment which is for the time being or has (before or after the passing of this Act) been in force in any part of the United Kingdom and Islands.

(5) Nothing in this section shall be taken to exclude the operation of section 3(8) above in relation to an exemption under this section.

Exceptions for seamen, aircrews and other special cases.

8.—(1) Where a person arrives at a place in the United Kingdom as a member of the crew of a ship or aircraft under an engagement requiring him to leave on that ship as a member of the crew, or to leave within seven days on that or another aircraft as a member of its crew, then unless either—

(a) there is in force a deportation order made against him; or

(b) he has at any time been refused leave to enter the United Kingdom and has not since then been given leave to enter or remain in the United Kingdom; or

(c) an immigration officer requires him to submit to examination in accordance with Schedule 2 to this Act;

he may without leave enter the United Kingdom at that place and remain until the departure of the ship or aircraft on which he is required by his engagement to leave.

(2) The Secretary of State may by order exempt any person or class of persons, either unconditionally or subject to such conditions as may be imposed by or under the order, from all or any of the provisions of this Act relating to those who are not British citizens.

An order under this subsection, if made with respect to a class of persons shall be made by statutory instrument, which shall be subject to annulment in pursuance of a resolution of either House of Parliament.

(3) The provisions of this Act relating to those who are not British Citizens shall not apply to any person so long as he is a member of a mission (within the meaning of the Diplomatic Privileges Act 1964), a person who is a member of the family and forms part of the household of such a member, or a person otherwise entitled to the like immunity from jurisdiction as is conferred by that Act on a diplomatic agent.

(4) The provisions of this Act relating to those who are not British citizens, other than the provisions relating to deportation, shall also not apply to any person so long as either—

(a) he is subject, as a member of the home forces, to service law; or

(b) being a member of a Commonwealth force or of a force raised under the law of any associated state, colony, protectorate or protected state, is undergoing or about to undergo training in the United Kingdom with any body, contingent or detachment of the home forces; or

(c) he is serving or posted for service in the United Kingdom as a member of a visiting force or of any force raised as aforesaid or as a member of an international headquarters or defence organisation designated for the time being by an Order in Council under section 1 of the International Headquarters and Defence Organisation Act 1964.

(5) Where a person having a limited leave to enter or remain in the United Kingdom becomes entitled to an exemption under this section, that leave shall continue to apply after he ceases to be entitled to the exemption, unless it has by then expired; and a person is not to be regarded for purposes of this Act as having been settled in the United Kingdom at any time when he was entitled under the former immigration laws to any exemption corresponding to any of those afford by subsection (3) or (4)(b) or (c) above or by any order under subsection (2) above.

(5A) An order under subsection (2) above may, as regards any person or class of persons to whom it applies, provide for that person or class to be in specified circumstances regarded (notwithstanding the order) as settled in the United Kingdom for the purposes of section 1(1) of the British Nationality Act 1981.

(6) In this section "the home forces" means any of Her Majesty's forces other than a Commonwealth force or a force raised under the law of any associated state, colony, protectorate or protected state; "Commonwealth force" means a force of any country to which provisions of the Visiting Forces Act 1952 apply without an Order in Council under section 1 of the Act; and "visiting force" means a body, contingent or detachment of the forces of a country to which any of those provisions apply, being a body, contingent or detachment for the time being present in the United Kingdom on the invitation of Her Majesty's Government in the United Kingdom.

Further provisions as to common travel area

9.—(1) Subject to subsection (5) below, the provisions of Schedule 4 to this Act shall have effect for the purpose of taking account in the United Kingdom of the operation in any of the Islands of the immigration laws there.

(2) Persons who lawfully enter the United Kingdom on a local journey from a place in the common travel area after having either—

(a) entered any of the Islands or the Republic of Ireland on coming from a place outside the common travel area; or

(b) left the United Kingdom while having a limited leave to enter or remain which has since expired;

if they are not British citizens (and are not to be regarded under Schedule 4 to this Act as having leave to enter the United Kingdom), shall be subject in the United Kingdom to such restrictions on the period for which they may remain, and such conditions restricting their employment or occupation or requiring them to register with the police or both, as may be imposed by an order of the Secretary of State and may be applicable to them.

(3) Any provision of this Act applying to a limited leave or to conditions attached to a limited leave shall, unless otherwise provided, have effect in relation to a person subject to any restriction or condition by virtue of an order under subsection (2) above as if the provisions of the order applicable to him were terms on which he had been given leave under this Act to enter the United Kingdom.

(4) Section 1(3) above shall not be taken to affect the operation of a deportation order; and, subject to Schedule 4 to this Act, a person who is not a British citizen may not by virtue of section 1(3) enter the United Kingdom without leave on a local journey from a place in the common travel area if either—

(a) he is on arrival in the United Kingdom given written notice by an immigration officer stating that, the Secretary of State having issued directions for him not to be given entry to the United Kingdom on the ground that his exclusion is conducive to the public good as being in the interests of national security, he is accordingly refused leave to enter the United Kingdom; or

(b) he has at any time been refused leave to enter the United Kingdom and has not since then been given leave to enter or remain in the United Kingdom.

(5) If it appears to Secretary of State necessary so to do by reason of differences between the immigration laws of the United Kingdom and any of the Islands, he may by order exclude that island from section 1(3) above for such purposes as may be specified in the order, and references in this Act to the Islands shall apply to an island so excluded so far only as may be provided by order of the Secretary of State.

(6) The Secretary of State shall also have power by order to exclude the Republic of Ireland from section 1(3) for such purposes as may be specified in the order.

(7) An order of the Secretary of State under this section shall be made by statutory instrument, which shall be subject to annulment in pursuance of a resolution of either House of Parliament.

Entry otherwise than by sea or air.

10.—(1) Her Majesty may by Order in Council direct that any of the provisions of this Act shall have effect in relation to persons entering or seeking to enter the United Kingdom on arrival otherwise than by ship or aircraft as they have effect in the case of a person arriving by ship or aircraft; and any such Order may make such adaptations or modifications of those provisions, and such provisions supplementary thereto, as appear to Her Majesty to be necessary or expedient for the purposes of the Order.

(2) The provision made by an Order in Council under this section may include provision for excluding the Republic of Ireland from section 1(3) of this Act either generally or for any specified purposes.

(3) No recommendation shall be made to Her Majesty to make an Order in Council under this section unless a draft of the Order has been laid before Parliament and approved by a resolution of each House of Parliament.

Construction of references to entry, and other phrases relating to travel.

11.—(1) A person arriving in the United Kingdom by ship or aircraft shall for purposes of this Act be deemed not to enter the United Kingdom unless and until he disembarks, and on disembarkation at a port shall further be deemed not to enter the United Kingdom so long as he remains in such area (if any) at the port as may be approved for this purpose by an immigration officer; and a person who has not otherwise entered the United Kingdom shall be deemed not to do so as long as he is detained, or temporarily admitted or released while liable to detention, under the powers conferred by Schedule 2 to this Act.

(2) In this Act "disembark" means disembark from a ship or aircraft, and "embark" means embark in a ship or aircraft; and, except in subsection (1) above,—

(a) references to disembarking in the United Kingdom do not apply to disembarking after a local journey from a place in the United Kingdom or elsewhere in the common travel area; and

(b) references to embarking in the United Kingdom do not apply to embarking for a local journey to a place in the United Kingdom or elsewhere in the common travel area.

(3) Except in so far as the context otherwise requires, references in this Act to arriving in the United Kingdom by ship shall extend to arrival by any floating structure, and "disembark" shall be construed accordingly; but the provisions of this Act specially relating to members of the crew of a ship shall not by virtue of this provision apply in relation to any floating structure not being a ship.

(4) For purposes of this Act "common travel area" has the meaning given by section 1(3), and a journey is, in relation to the common travel area, a local journey if but only if it begins and ends in the common travel area and is not made by a ship or aircraft which—

(a) in the case of a journey to a place in the United Kingdom, began its voyage from, or has during its voyage called at, a place not in the common travel area; or

(b) in the case of a journey from a place in the United Kingdom, is due to end its voyage in, or call in the course of its voyage at, a place not in the common travel area.

(5) A person who enters the United Kingdom lawfully by virtue of section 8(1) above, and seeks to remain beyond the time limited by section 8(1), shall be treated for purposes of this Act as seeking to enter the United Kingdom.

PART II

APPEALS

The appellate authorities

Immigration Appeal Tribunal and adjudicators

12.—The Immigration Appeal Tribunal and adjudicators provided for by the Immigration Appeals Act 1969 shall continue for purposes of this Act, and—

(a) members of the Tribunal shall continue to be appointed by the Lord Chancellor and adjudicators by the Secretary of State; and

(b) the provisions of Schedule 1 to that Act shall continue to apply as set out in Schedule 5 to this Act with the required adaptation of references to that Act, but with the substitution also of references to the Minister for the Civil Service for references to the Treasury.

Appeals to adjudicator or Tribunal in first instance

Appeals against exclusion from United Kingdom.

13—(1) Subject to the provisions of this Part of this Act, a person who is refused leave to enter the United Kingdom under this Act may appeal to an adjudicator against the decision that he requires leave or against the refusal.

(2) Subject to the provisions of this Part of this Act, a person who, on an application duly made, is refused a certificate of entitlement or an entry clearance may appeal to an adjudicator against the refusal.

(3) A person within section 3(9) above who does not hold a certificate of entitlement shall not be entitled to appeal on the ground that he has the right of abode in the United Kingdom

against a decision that he requires leave to enter the United Kingdom unless—

(a) he claims to be a British citizen and produces (or is present when there is produced) a United Kingdom passport describing him as such a citizen or a United Kingdom passport describing him as a citizen of the United Kingdom and Colonies having the right of abode in the United Kingdom; or

(b) in the case of such a woman as is mentioned in paragraph (b) of section 3(9) above, she shows that immediately before the commencement of the British Nationality Act 1981 she satisfied the conditions specified in sub-paragraphs (i) and (ii) of that paragraph;

and a person shall not be entitled to appeal against a refusal of leave to enter so long as he is in the United Kingdom, unless he was refused leave at a port of entry and at a time when he held a current entry clearance or was a person named in a current work permit.

(4) An appeal against a refusal of leave to enter shall be dismissed by the adjudicator if he is satisfied that the appellant was at the time of the refusal an illegal entrant, and an appeal against a refusal of an entry clearance shall be dismissed by the adjudicator if he is satisfied that a deportation order was at the time of the refusal in force in respect of the appellant.

(5) A person shall not be entitled to appeal against a refusal of leave to enter, or against a refusal of an entry clearance, if the Secretary of State certifies that directions have been given by the Secretary of State (and not by a person acting under his authority) for the appellant not to be given entry to the United Kingdom on the ground that his exclusion is conducive to the public good, or if the leave to enter or entry clearance was refused in obedience to any such directions.

Appeals against conditions

14.—(1) Subject to the provisions of this Part of this Act, a person who has a limited leave under this Act to enter or remain in the United Kingdom may appeal to an adjudicator against any variation of the leave (whether as regards duration or conditions), or against any refusal to vary it; and a variation shall not take effect so long as an appeal is pending under this subsection against the variation, nor shall an appellant be required to leave the United Kingdom by reason of the expiration of his leave so long as his appeal is pending under this subsection against a refusal to enlarge or remove the limit on the duration of the leave.

(2) Subject to the provisions of this Part of this Act, a person who, on ceasing to be entitled to an exemption under any

provision of section 8 above other than section 8(1), or on ceasing while in the United Kingdom to be a British citizen, is given a limited leave to remain may appeal to an adjudicator against any provision limiting the duration of the leave or attaching a condition to it; and so long as an appeal is pending under this subsection against any provision, effect shall not be given to that provision.

(3) A person shall not be entitled to appeal under subsection (1) above against any variation of his leave which reduces its duration, or against any refusal to enlarge or remove the limit on its duration, if the Secretary of State certifies that the appellant's departure from the United Kingdom would be conducive to the public good, as being in the interests of national security or of the relations between the United Kingdom and any other country or for other reasons of a political nature, or the decision questioned by the appeal was taken on that ground by the Secretary of State (and not by a person acting under his authority).

(4) A person shall not be entitled to appeal under subsection (1) above against any variation made by statutory instrument, or against any refusal of the Secretary of State to make a statutory instrument.

Appeals in respect of deportation orders

15.—(1) Subject to the provisions of this Part of this Act, a person may appeal to an adjudicator against—

(a) a decision of the Secretary of State to make a deportation order against him by virtue of section 3(5) above; or

(b) a refusal by the Secretary of State to revoke a deportation order made against him.

(2) A deportation order shall not be made against a person by virtue of section 3(5) above so long as an appeal may be brought against the decision to make it nor, if such an appeal is duly brought, so long as the appeal is pending; but, in calculating the period of eight weeks limited by section 5(3) above for making a deportation order against a person as belonging to the family of another person, there shall be disregarded any period during which there is pending an appeal against the decision to make it.

(3) A person shall not be entitled to appeal against a decision to make a deportation order against him if the ground of the decision was that his deportation is conducive to the public good as being in the interests of national security or of the relations between the United Kingdom and any other country or for other reasons of a political nature.

(4) A person shall not be entitled to appeal under this section against a refusal to revoke a deportation order, if the Secretary of State certifies that the appellant's exclusion from the United Kingdom is conducive to the public good or if revocation was

refused on that ground by the Secretary of State (and not by a person acting under his authority).

(5) A person shall not be entitled to appeal under this section against a refusal to revoke a deportation order so long as he is in the United Kingdom, whether because he has not complied with the requirement to leave or because he has contravened the prohibition on entering.

(6) On an appeal against a decision to make a deportation order against a person as belonging to the family of another person, or an appeal against a refusal to revoke a deportation order so made, the appellant shall not be allowed, for the purpose of showing that he does not or did not belong to another person's family, to dispute any statement made with a view to obtaining leave for the appellant to enter or remain in the United Kingdom (including any statement made to obtain an entry clearance) unless the appellant shows that the statement was not so made by him or by any person acting with his authority and that, when he took the benefit of the leave, he did not know any such statement had been made to obtain it or, if he did know, was under the age of eighteen.

(7) An appeal under this section shall be to the Appeal Tribunal in the first instance, instead of to an adjudicator, if—

(a) it is an appeal against a decision to make a deportation order and the ground of the decision was that the deportation of the appellant is conducive to the public good; or

(b) it is an appeal against a decision to make a deportation order against a person as belonging to the family of another person, or an appeal against a refusal to revoke a deportation order so made; or

(c) there is pending a related appeal to which paragraph (b) above applies.

(8) Where an appeal to an adjudicator is pending under this section, and before the adjudicator has begun to hear it a related appeal is brought the appeal to the adjudicator shall be dealt with instead by the Appeal Tribunal and be treated as an appeal duly made to the Tribunal in the first instance.

(9) In relation to an appeal under this section in respect of a deportation order against any person (whether an appeal against a decision to make or against a refusal to revoke the order), any other appeal under this section is a 'related appeal' if it is an appeal in respect of a deportation order against another person as belonging to the family of the first-mentioned person.

16.—(1) Subject to the provisions of this Part of this Act, where directions are given under this Act for a person's removal from the United Kingdom either—

Appeals against validity of directions for removal

(a) on the ground that he is an illegal entrant or on the ground specifically that he has entered the United Kingdom in breach of a deportation order; or

(b) under the special powers conferred by Schedule 2 to this Act in relation to members of the crew of a ship or aircraft or persons coming to the United Kingdom to join a ship or aircraft as a member of the crew;

then he may appeal to an adjudicator against those directions on the ground that in the facts of his case there was in law no power to give them on the ground on which they were given.

(2) A person shall not be entitled to appeal under this section so long as he is in the United Kingdom, unless he is appealing against directions given by virtue of a deportation order (whether on the ground specifically that he has returned in breach of that order or on the ground that he is an illegal entrant) and is appealing on the ground that he is not the person named in that order.

(3) Where a person appeals under this section against directions given by virtue of a deportation order, he shall not be allowed to dispute the original validity of that order.

(4) An appeal under this section against directions given as mentioned in subsection (1)(b) shall be dismissed by the adjudicator, notwithstanding that the ground of appeal may be made out, if he is satisfied that there was power to give the like directions on the ground that the appellant was an illegal entrant.

17.—(1) Subject to the provisions of this Part of this Act, where directions are given under this Act for a person's removal from the United Kingdom either—

Appeals against removal on objection to destination

(a) on his being refused leave to enter; or

(b) on a deportation order being made against him; or

(c) on his having entered the United Kingdom in breach of a deportation order;

he may appeal to an adjudicator against the directions on the ground that he ought to be removed (if at all) to a different country or territory specified by him.

(2) Where a person appeals under section 13(1) above on being refused leave to enter the United Kingdom, and either—

(a) before he does so, directions have been given for his removal from the United Kingdom to any country or territory; or

(b) before or after he does so, the Secretary of State or an immigration officer serves on him notice that any directions which may be given for his removal by virtue of the refusal will be for his removal to a country or territory or one of several countries or territories specified in the notice;

then he may on that appeal object to the country or territory to which he would be removed in pursuance of the directions, or to that specified in the notice (or to one or more of those specified), and claim that he ought to be removed (if at all) to a different country or territory specified by him.

(3) Where a person appeals under section 15 above against a decision to make a deportation order against him, and before or after he does so the Secretary of State serves on him notice that any directions which may be given for his removal by virtue of the deportation order will be for his removal to a country or territory or one of several countries or territories specified in the notice, then he may on that appeal object to the country or territory specified in the notice (or to one or more of those specified), and claim that he ought to be removed (if at all) to a different country or territory specified by him.

(4) Where by virtue of subsection (2) or (3) above a person is able to object to a country or territory on an appeal under section 13(1) or 15, and either he does not object to it on that appeal or his objection to it on that appeal is not sustained, then he shall not be entitled to appeal under this section against any directions subsequently given by virtue of the refusal or order in question, if their effect will be his removal to that country or territory.

(5) A person shall not be entitled to appeal under this section against any directions given on his being refused leave to enter the United Kingdom, unless either he is also appealing under section 13(1) against the decision that he requires leave to enter or he was refused leave at a port of entry and at a time when he held a current entry clearance or was a person named in a current work permit.

Notice of matters in respect of which there are rights of appeal

18.—(1) The Secretary of State may by regulations provide—

(a) for written notice to be given to a person of any such decision or action taken in respect of him as is appealable under this Part of this Act (whether or not he is in the facts of his case entitled to appeal) or would be so appealable but for the ground on which it is taken;

(b) for any such notice to include a statement of the reasons for the decision or action and, where the action is the giving of directions for the removal of any person from the United Kingdom, of the country or territory to which he is to be removed;

(c) for any such notice to be accompanied by a statement

containing particulars of the rights of appeal available under this Part of this Act and of the procedure by which those rights may be exercised;

(d) for the form of any such notice or statement and the way in which a notice is to be or may be given.

(2) For the purpose of any proceedings under this Part of this Act a statement including a notice in pursuance of regulations under this section shall be conclusive of the person by whom and of the ground on which any decision or action was taken.

(3) The power to make regulations under this section shall be exercisable by statutory instrument, and any statutory instrument containing such regulations shall be subject to annulment in pursuance of a resolution of either House of Parliament.

Determination of appeals by adjudicators

19.—(1) Subject to sections 13(4) and 16(4) above, and to any restriction on the grounds of appeal, an adjudicator on an appeal to him under this Part of this Act—

(a) shall allow the appeal if he considers—

(i) that the decision or action against which the appeal is brought was not in accordance with the law or with any immigration rules applicable to the case; or

(ii) where the decision or action involved the exercise of a discretion by the Secretary of State or an officer, that the discretion should have been exercised differently; and

(b) in any other case, shall dismiss the appeal.

(2) For the purposes of subsection (1)(a) above the adjudicator may review any determination of a question of fact on which the decision or action was based; and for the purposes of subsection (1)(a)(ii) no decision or action which is in accordance with the immigration rules shall be treated as having involved the exercise of a discretion by the Secretary of State by reason only of the fact that he has been requested by or on behalf of the appellant to depart, or to authorise an officer to depart, from the rules and has refused to do so.

(3) Where an appeal is allowed, the adjudicator shall give such directions for giving effect to the determination as the adjudicator thinks requisite, and may also make recommendations with respect to any other action which the adjudicator considers should be taken in the case under this Act; and, subject to section 20(2) below, it shall be the duty of the Secretary of State and of any officer to whom directions are given under this subsection to comply with them.

(4) Where in accordance with section 15 above a person appeals to the Appeal Tribunal in the first instance, this section

shall apply with the substitution of references to the Tribunal for references to an adjudicator.

Appeals from adjudicator to Tribunal, and review of decisions

20.—(1) Subject to any requirement of rules of procedure as to leave to appeal, any party to an appeal to an adjudicator may, if dissatisfied with his determination thereon, appeal to the Appeal Tribunal, and the Tribunal may affirm the determination or make any other determination which could have been made by the adjudicator. Appeal to Tribunal from determination of adjudicator

(2) Directions given by an adjudicator under section 19(3) above need not be complied with so long as an appeal can be brought against his determination and, if such an appeal is duly brought, so long as the appeal is pending; and if the Tribunal affirm his determination allowing the appeal, they may alter or add to his directions and recommendations under section 19(3) or replace them with their own directions and recommendations, and the provisions of that subsection shall apply to directions given by them accordingly.

(3) Where an appeal is dismissed by an adjudicator but allowed by the Tribunal, section 19(3) above shall apply with the substitution of references to the Tribunal for references to the adjudicator.

21.—(1) Where in any case— Reference of cases for further consideration

(a) an adjudicator has dismissed an appeal, and there has been no further appeal to the Appeal Tribunal, or the Tribunal has dismissed an appeal made to them in the first instance by virtue of section 15 above; or

(b) the Appeal Tribunal has affirmed the determination of an adjudicator dismissing an appeal, or reversed the determination of an adjudicator allowing an appeal;

the Secretary of State may at any time refer for consideration under this section any matter relating to the case which was not before the adjudicator or Tribunal.

(2) Any reference under this section shall be to an adjudicator or to the Appeal Tribunal, and the adjudicator or Tribunal shall consider the matter which is the subject of the reference and report to the Secretary of State the opinion of the adjudicator or Tribunal thereon.

Supplementary

22.—(1) The Secretary of State may make rules (in this Act referred to as "rules of procedure")— Procedure

(a) for regulating the exercise of the rights of appeal conferred by this Part of this Act;

(b) for prescribing the practice and procedure to be followed on or in connection with appeals thereunder, including the mode and burden of proof and admissibility of evidence on such an appeal; and

(c) for other matters preliminary or incidental to or arising out of such appeals, including proof of the decisions of adjudicators or the Appeal Tribunal.

(2) Rules of procedure may include provision—

(a) enabling the Tribunal, on an appeal from an adjudicator, to remit the appeal to an adjudicator for determination by him in accordance with any directions of the Tribunal, or for further evidence to be obtained with a view to determination by the Tribunal; or

(b) enabling any functions of the Tribunal which relate to matters preliminary or incidental to an appeal, or which are conferred by Part II of Schedule 2 to this Act, to be performed by a single member of the Tribunal; or

(c) conferring on adjudicators or the Tribunal such ancillary powers as the Secretary of State thinks necessary for the purposes of the exercise of their functions.

(3) The rules of procedure shall provide that any appellant shall have the right to be legally represented.

(4) Where on an appeal under this Part of this Act it is alleged—

(a) that a passport or other travel document, certificate of entitlement entry clearance or work permit (or any part thereof or entry therein) on which a party relies is a forgery; and

(b) that the disclosure to that party of any matters relating to the method of detection would be contrary to the public interest;

then (without prejudice to the generality of the power to make rules of procedure) the adjudicator or Tribunal shall arrange for the proceedings to take place in the absence of that party and his representatives while the allegation at (b) above is inquired into by the adjudicator or Tribunal and, if it appears to the adjudicator or Tribunal that the allegation is made out, for such further period as appears necessary in order to ensure that those matters can be presented to the adjudicator or Tribunal without any disclosure being directly or indirectly made contrary to the public interest.

(5) If under the rules of procedure leave to appeal to the Tribunal is required in cases where an adjudicator dismisses an appeal under section 13 above, then the authority having power to grant leave to appeal shall grant it—

(a) in any case where the appeal was against a decision that the appellant required leave to enter the United Kingdom, and the authority is satisfied that at the time of the decision he held a certificate of entitlement; and

(b) in any case where the appeal was against a refusal of leave to enter, and the authority is satisfied that at the time of the refusal the appellant held an entry clearance and that the dismissal of the appeal was not required by section 13(4).

(6) A person who is required under or in accordance with rules of procedure to attend and give evidence or produce documents before an adjudicator or the Tribunal, and fails without reasonable excuse to comply with the requirement, shall be guilty of an offence and liable on summary conviction to a fine not exceeding £100.

(7) The power to make rules of procedure shall be exercisable by statutory instrument, which shall be subject to annulment in pursuance of a resolution of either House of Parliament.

23.—The Secretary of State may with the consent of the Treasury make grants to any voluntary organisation which provides advice or assistance for, or other services for the welfare of, persons who have rights of appeal under this Part of this Act.

Financial support for organisations helping persons with rights of appeal.

PART III

CRIMINAL PROCEEDINGS

24.—(1) A person who is not a British citizen shall be guilty of an offence punishable on summary conviction with a fine of not more than £200 or with imprisonment for not more than six months, or with both, in any of the following cases:

Illegal entry and similar offences.

(a) if contrary to this Act he knowingly enters the United Kingdom in breach of a deportation order or without leave;

(b) if, having only a limited leave to enter or remain in the United Kingdom, he knowingly either—
  (i) remains beyond the time limited by the leave; or
  (ii) fails to observe a condition of the leave;

(c) if, having lawfully entered the United Kingdom without leave by virtue of section 8(1) above, he remains without leave beyond the time allowed by section 8(1);

(d) if, without reasonable excuse, he fails to comply with any requirement imposed on him under Schedule 2 to this Act to report to a medical officer of health or the chief administrative medical officer of a Health and Social

Services Board, or to attend, or submit to a test or examination, as required by such an officer;

(e) if, without reasonable excuse, he fails to observe any restriction imposed on him under Schedule 2 or 3 to this Act as to residence or as to reporting to the police or to an immigration officer;

(f) if he disembarks in the United Kingdom from a ship or aircraft after being placed on board under Schedule 2 or 3 to this Act with a view to his removal from the United Kingdom;

(g) if he embarks in contravention of a restriction imposed by or under an Order in Council under section 3(7) of this Act.

(2) A constable or immigration officer may arrest without warrant anyone who has, or whom he, with reasonable cause, suspects to have, committed or attempted to commit an offence under this section other than an offence under subsection (1)(d) above.

(3) The extended time limit for prosecutions which is provided for by section 28 below shall apply to offences under subsection (1)(a), (b)(i) and (c) above.

(4) In proceedings for an offence against subsection (1)(a) above of entering the United Kingdom without leave,—

(a) any stamp purporting to have been imprinted on a passport or other travel document by an immigration officer on a particular date for the purpose of giving leave shall be presumed to have been duly so imprinted, unless the contrary is proved;

(b) proof that a person had leave to enter the United Kingdom shall lie on the defence if, but only if, he is shown to have entered within six months before the date when the proceedings were commenced.

Assisting illegal entry, and harbouring.

25.—(1) Any person knowingly concerned in making or carrying out arrangements for securing or facilitating the entry into the United Kingdom of anyone whom he knows or has reasonable cause for believing to be an illegal entrant shall be guilty of an offence, punishable on summary conviction with a fine of not more than £400 or with imprisonment for not more than six months, or with both, or on conviction on indictment with a fine or with imprisonment for not more than seven years, or with both.

(2) Without prejudice to subsection (1) above a person knowingly harbouring anyone whom he knows or has reasonable cause for believing to be either an illegal entrant or a person who has committed an offence under section 24(1)(b) or (c) above, shall be guilty of an offence, punishable on summary

conviction with a fine of not more than £400 or with imprisonment for not more than six months, or with both.

(3) An immigration officer may arrest without warrant anyone who has, or whom he, with reasonable cause, suspects to have, committed an offence under subsection (1) above.

(4) The extended time limit for prosecutions which is provided for by section 28 below shall apply to offences under this section.

(5) Subsection (1) above shall apply to things done outside as well as to things done in the United Kingdom where they are done—

(a) by a British citizen, a British Dependent Territories citizen, or a British Overseas citizen;
(b) by a person who under the British Nationality Act 1981 is a British subject; or
(c) by a British protected person (within the meaning of that Act).

(6) Where a person convicted on indictment of an offence under subsection (1) above is at the time of the offence—

(a) the owner or one of the owners of a ship, aircraft or vehicle used or intended to be used in carrying out the arrangements in respect of which the offence is committed; or
(b) a director or manager of a company which is the owner or one of the owners of any such ship, aircraft or vehicle; or
(c) captain of any such ship or aircraft;

then subject to subsections (7) and (8) below the court before which he is convicted may order the forfeiture of the ship, aircraft or vehicle.

In this subsection (but not in subsection (7) below) "owner" in relation to a ship, aircraft or vehicle which is the subject of a hire-purchase agreement, includes the person in possession of it under that agreement and, in relation to a ship or aircraft, includes a charterer.

(7) A court shall not order a ship or aircraft to be forfeited under subsection (6) above on a person's conviction, unless—

(a) in the case of a ship, it is of less than 500 tons gross tonnage or, in the case of an aircraft (not being a hovercraft), it is of less than 5,700 kilogrammes operating weight; or
(b) the person convicted is at the time of the offence the owner or one of the owners, or a director or manager of a company which is the owner or one of the owners, of the ship or aircraft; or
(c) the ship or aircraft, under the arrangements in respect of which the offence is committed, has been used for bringing more than 20 persons at one time to the United Kingdom as illegal entrants, and the intention to use the ship or aircraft

in bringing persons to the United Kingdom as illegal entrants was known to, or could by the exercise of reasonable diligence, have been discovered by, some person on whose conviction the ship or aircraft would have been liable to forfeiture in accordance with paragraph (b) above.

In this subsection "operating weight" means in relation to an aircraft the maximum total weight of the aircraft and its contents at which the aircraft may take off anywhere in the world, in the most favourable circumstances, in accordance with the certificate of airworthiness in force in respect of the aircraft.

(8) A court shall not order a ship, aircraft or vehicle to be forfeited under subsection (6) above, where a person claiming to be the owner of the ship, aircraft or vehicle or otherwise interested in it applies to be heard by the court, unless an opportunity has been given to him to show cause why the order should not be made.

General offences in connection with administration of Act.

26.—(1) A person shall be guilty of an offence punishable on summary conviction with a fine of not more than £200 or with imprisonment for not more than six months, or with both, in any of the following cases—

(a) if, without reasonable excuse, he refuses or fails to submit to examination under Schedule 2 to this Act;

(b) if, without reasonable excuse, he refuses or fails to furnish or produce any information in his possession, or any documents in his possession or control, which he is on an examination under that Schedule required to furnish or produce;

(c) if on any such examination or otherwise he makes or causes to be made to an immigration officer or other person lawfully acting in the execution of this Act a return, statement or representation which he knows to be false or does not believe to be true;

(d) if, without lawful authority, he alters any certificate of entitlement, entry clearance, work permit or other document issued or made under or for the purposes of this Act, or uses for the purposes of this Act, or has in his possession for such use, any passport, certificate of entitlement, entry clearance, work permit or other document which he knows or has reasonable cause to believe to be false;

(e) if, without reasonable excuse, he fails to complete and produce a landing or embarkation card in accordance with any order under Schedule 2 to this Act;

(f) if, without reasonable excuse, he fails to comply with any requirement of regulations under section 4(3) or of an order under section 4(4) above;

(g) if, without reasonable excuse, he obstructs an immigration officer or other person lawfully acting in the execution of this Act.

(2) The extended time limit for prosecutions which is provided for by section 28 below shall apply to offences under subsection (1)(c) and (d) above.

Offences by persons connected with ships or aircraft or with ports.

27.—A person shall be guilty of an offence punishable on summary conviction with a fine of not more than £200 or with imprisonment for not more than six months, or with both, in any of the following cases—

(a) if, being the captain of a ship or aircraft,—

(i) he knowingly permits a person to disembark in the United Kingdom when required under Schedule 2 or 3 to this Act to prevent it, or fails without reasonable excuse to take any steps he is required by or under Schedule 2 to take in connection with the disembarkation or examination of passengers or for furnishing a passenger list or particulars of members of the crew; or

(ii) he fails, without reasonable excuse, to comply with any directions given him under Schedule 2 or 3 with respect to the removal of a person from the United Kingdom;

(b) if, as owner or agent of a ship or aircraft,—

(i) he arranges, or is knowingly concerned in any arrangements, for the ship or aircraft to call at a port other than a port of entry contrary to any provision of Schedule 2 to this Act; or

(ii) he fails, without reasonable excuse, to take any steps required by an order under Schedule 2 for the supply to passengers of landing or embarkation cards; or

(iii) he fails, without reasonable excuse, to make arrangements for the removal of a person from the United Kingdom when required to do so by directions given under Schedule 2 or 3 to this Act;

(c) if, as owner or agent of a ship or aircraft or as a person concerned in the management of a port, he fails, without reasonable excuse, to take any steps required by Schedule 2 in relation to the embarkation or disembarkation of passengers where a control area is designated.

Proceedings

28.—(1) Where the offence is one to which, under section 24, 25 or 26 above, an extended time limit for prosecutions is to apply, then—

(a) an information relating to the offence, may in England and Wales be tried by a magistrates' court if it is laid within six months after the commission of the offence, or if it is laid within three years after the commission of the offence and not more than two months after the date certified by a chief officer of police to be the date on which evidence sufficient to justify proceedings came to the notice of an officer of his police force; and

(b) summary proceedings for the offence may in Scotland be commenced within six months after the commission of the offence, or within three years after the commission of the offence and not more than two months after the date on which evidence sufficient in the opinion of the Lord Advocate to justify proceedings came to his knowledge; and

(c) a complaint charging the commission of the offence may in Northern Ireland be heard and determined by a magistrates' court if it is made within six months after the commission of the offence, or if it is made within three years after the commission of the offence and not more than two months after the date certified by an officer of police not below the rank of assistant chief constable to be the date on which evidence sufficient to justify the proceedings came to the notice of the police in Northern Ireland.

(2) For the purposes of subsection (1)(b) above proceedings shall be deemed to be commenced on the date on which a warrant to apprehend or to cite the accused is granted, if such warrant is executed without undue delay; and a certificate of the Lord Advocate as to the date on which such evidence as is mentioned in subsection (1)(b) came to his knowledge shall be conclusive evidence.

(3) For the purposes of the trial of a person for an offence under this Part of this Act, the offence shall be deemed to have been committed either at the place at which it actually was committed or at any place at which he may be.

(4) Any powers exercisable under this Act in the case of any person may be exercised notwithstanding that proceedings for an offence under this Part of this Act have been taken against him.

Contributions for expenses of persons returning abroad.

29.—(1) The Secretary of State may, in such cases as he may with the approval of the Treasury determine, make payments of such amount as may be so determined to meet or provide for expenses of persons who are not British citizens in leaving the

United Kingdom for a country or territory where they intend to reside permanently, including travelling expenses for members of their families or households.

(2) The Secretary of State shall, so far as practicable, administer this section so as to secure that a person's expenses in leaving the United Kingdom are not met by or out of a payment made by the Secretary of State unless it is shown that it is in that person's interest to leave the United Kingdom and that he wishes to do so.

[Section 30 was repealed by the Mental Health (Scotland) Act 1984.]

31.—There shall be defrayed out of moneys provided by Parliament any expenses incurred by a Secretary of State under or by virtue of this Act— Expenses.

(a) by way of administrative expenses; or

(b) in connection with the removal of any person from the United Kingdom under Schedule 2 or 3 to this Act or the departure with him of his dependants, or his or their maintenance pending departure; or

(c) on account of the remuneration, allowances and other sums payable to or in respect of the adjudicators and members of the Immigration Appeal Tribunal, or of the remuneration of the officers and servants appointed for the adjudicators or Tribunal, or of the expenses of the adjudicators or Tribunal; or

(d) on the making of any grants or payments under section 23 or 29 above.

32.—(1) Any power conferred by Part I of this Act to make an Order in Council or order (other than a deportation order) or to give any directions includes power to revoke or vary the Order in Council, order or directions. General provisions as to Orders in Council, etc.

(2) Any documents purporting to be an order, notice or direction made or given by the Secretary of State for the purposes of this Act and to be signed by him or on his behalf, and any documents purporting to be a certificate of the Secretary of State so given and to be signed by him, shall be received in evidence, and shall, until the contrary is proved, be deemed to be made or issued by him.

(3) Prima facie evidence of any such order, notice, direction or certificate as aforesaid may, in any legal proceedings or proceedings under Part II of this Act, be given by the production

of a document bearing a certificate purporting to be signed by or on behalf of the Secretary of State and stating that the document is a true copy of the order, notice, direction or certificate.

(4) Where an order under section 8(2) above applies to persons specified in a schedule to the order, or any directions of the Secretary of State given for the purposes of this Act apply to persons specified in a schedule to the directions, prima facie evidence of the provisions of the order or directions other than the schedule and of any entry contained in the schedule may, in any legal proceedings or proceedings under Part II of this Act, be given by the production of a document purporting to be signed by or on behalf of the Secretary of State and stating that the document is a true copy of the said provisions and of the relevant entry.

33.—(1) For purposes of this Act, except in so far as the context otherwise requires— Interpretation.

"aircraft" includes hovercraft, "airport" includes hoverport and "port" includes airport;

"captain" means master (of a ship) or commander (of an aircraft);

"certificate of entitlement" means such a certificate as is referred to in section 3(9) above;

"crew", in relation to a ship or aircraft, means all persons actually employed in the working or service of the ship or aircraft, including the captain, and "member of the crew" shall be construed accordingly;

"entrant" means a person entering or seeking to enter the United Kingdom, and "illegal entrant" means a person unlawfully entering or seeking to enter in breach of a deportation order or of the immigration laws, and includes also a person who has so entered;

"entry clearance" means a visa, entry certificate or other document which, in accordance with the immigration rules, is to be taken as evidence of a person's eligibility, though not a British citizen, for entry into the United Kingdom (but does not include a work permit);

"immigration laws" means this Act and any law for purposes similar to this Act which is for the time being or has (before or after the passing of this Act) been in force in any part of the United Kingdom and Islands;

"immigration rules" means the rules for the time being laid down as mentioned in section 3(2) above;

"the Islands" means the Channel Islands and the Isle of Man, and "the United Kingdom and Islands" means the

United Kingdom and the Islands taken together;

"legally adopted" means adopted in pursuance of an order made by any court in the United Kingdom and Islands or by any adoption specified as an overseas adoption by order of the Secretary of State under section 4 of the Adoption Act 1968;

"limited leave" and "indefinite leave" mean respectively leave under this Act to enter or remain in the United Kingdom which is, and one which is not, limited as to duration;

"settled" shall be construed in accordance with subsection (2A) below;

"ship" includes every description of vessel used in navigation;

"United Kingdom passport" means a current passport issued by the Government of the United Kingdom, or by the Lieutenant-Governor of any of the Islands, or by the Government of any territory which is for the time being a dependent territory within the meaning of the British Nationality Act 1981;

"work permit" means a permit indicating, in accordance with the immigration rules, that a person named in it is eligible, though not a British citizen, for entry into the United Kingdom for the purpose of taking employment.

(2) It is hereby declared that, except as otherwise provided in this Act, a person is not to be treated for the purposes of any provision of this Act as ordinarily resident in the United Kingdom or in any of the Islands at a time when he is there in breach of the immigration laws.

(2A) Subject to section 8(5) above, references to a person being settled in the United Kingdom are references to his being ordinarily resident there without being subject under the immigration laws to any restriction on the period for which he may remain.

(3) The ports of entry for purposes of this Act, and the ports of exit for purposes of any Order in Council under section 3(7) above, shall be such ports as may from time to time be designated for the purpose by order of the Secretary of State made by statutory instrument.

(4) For purposes of this Act an appeal under Part II shall, subject to any express provision to the contrary, be treated as pending during the period beginning when notice of appeal is duly given and ending when the appeal is finally determined or withdrawn; and in the case of an appeal to an adjudicator, the appeal shall not be treated as finally determined so long as a further appeal can be brought by virtue of section 20 nor, if such

an appeal is duly brought, until it is determined or withdrawn.

(5) This Act shall not be taken to supersede or impair any power exercisable by Her Majesty in relation to aliens by virtue of Her prerogative.

Repeal, transitional and temporary.

34.—(1) Subject to the following provisions of this section, the enactments mentioned in Schedule 6 to this Act are hereby repealed, as from the coming into force of this Act, to the extent mentioned in column 3 of the Schedule; and—

(a) this Act, as from its coming into force, shall apply in relation to entrants or others arriving in the United Kingdom at whatever date before or after it comes into force; and

(b) after this Act comes into force anything done under or for the purposes of the former immigration laws shall have effect, in so far as any corresponding action could be taken under or for the purposes of this Act, as if done by way of action so taken, and in relation to anything so done this Act shall apply accordingly.

(2) Without prejudice to the generality of subsection (1)(a) and (b) above, a person refused leave to land by virtue of the Aliens Restriction Act 1914 shall be treated as having been refused leave to enter under this Act, and a person given leave to land by virtue of that Act shall be treated as having been given leave to enter under this Act; and similarly with the Commonwealth Immigrants Acts 1962 and 1968.

(3) A person treated in accordance with subsection (2) above as having leave to enter the United Kingdom—

(a) shall be treated as having an indefinite leave, if he is not at the coming into force of this Act subject to a condition limiting his stay in the United Kingdom; and

(b) shall be treated, if he is then subject to such a condition, as having a limited leave of such duration, and subject to such conditions (capable of being attached to leave under this Act), as correspond to the conditions to which he is then subject; but not to conditions not capable of being so attached.

This subsection shall have effect in relation to any restriction or requirement imposed by Order in Council under the Aliens Restriction Act 1914 as if it had been imposed by way of a landing condition.

(4) Notwithstanding anything in the foregoing provisions of this Act, the former immigration laws shall continue to apply, and this Act shall not apply,—

(a) in relation to the making of deportation orders and matters connected therewith in any case where a decision to make the order has been notified to the person concerned before the coming into force of this Act;

(b) in relation to removal from the United Kingdom and matters connected therewith (including detention pending removal or pending the giving of directions for removal) in any case where a person is to be removed in pursuance of a decision taken before the coming into force of this Act or in pursuance of a deportation order to the making of which paragraph (a) above applies;

(c) in relation to appeals against any decision taken or other thing done under the former immigration laws, whether taken or done before the coming into force of this Act or by virtue of this subsection.

(5) Subsection (1) above shall not be taken as empowering a court on appeal to recommend for deportation a person whom the court below could not recommend for deportation, or as affecting any right of appeal in respect of a recommendation for deportation made before this Act comes into force, or as enabling a notice given before this Act comes into force and not complying with section 6(2) to take the place of the notice required by section 6(2) to be given before a person is recommended for deportation.

(6) So long as section 2 of the Southern Rhodesia Act 1965 remains in force, this Act shall have effect subject to such provision as may (before or after this Act comes into force) be made by Order in Council under and for the purposes of that section.

Commencement, and interim provisions.

35.—(1) Except as otherwise provided by this Act, Parts I to III of this Act shall come into force on such day as the Secretary of State may appoint by order made by statutory instrument; and references to the coming into force of this Act shall be construed as references to the beginning of the day so appointed.

(2) Section 25 above, except section 25(2), and section 28 in its application to offences under section 25(1) shall come into force at the end of one month beginning with the date this Act is passed.

(3) The provisions of section 28(1) and (2) above shall have effect, as from the passing of this Act, in relation to offences under section 4A (unauthorised landing) of the Commonwealth Immigrants Act 1962 as amended by the Commonwealth Immigrants Act 1968, other than offences committed six months or more before the passing of this Act, as those provisions are expressed to have effect in relation to offences to which the extended time limit for prosecutions is to apply under section 24,

25 and 26 above; but where proceedings for an offence under section 4A of the Commonwealth Immigrants Act 1962 would have been out of time but for this subsection, section 4A(A) (under which, in certain cases, a person not producing a passport duly stamped by an immigration officer is presumed for purposes of that section to have landed in contravention of it, unless the contrary is proved) shall not apply.

(4) Section 1(2A)(d) of the Commonwealth Immigrants Act 1962 (which was inserted by section 1 of the Commonwealth Immigrants Act 1968, and excludes from the control on immigration under those Acts, among other persons, certain persons registered in the United Kingdom or in an independent country of the Commonwealth as citizens of the United Kingdom and Colonies) shall not apply—

(a) to a woman registered after the passing of this Act under or by virtue of section 6(2) (wives) of the British Nationality Act 1948, unless so registered either—

   (i) by virtue of her marriage to a citizen of the United Kingdom and Colonies before the passing of this Act; or

   (ii) by virtue of her marriage to such a citizen who at the time of her registration or at his death before that time was excluded from the control on immigration under the Commonwealth Immigrants Act 1962 and 1968 by section 1(2) of the 1962 Act; nor

(b) to anyone registered after the passing of this Act under or by virtue of section 7 (children) of the British Nationality Act 1948, unless so registered in the United Kingdom.

(5) So much of section 1 of the Aliens Restriction (Amendment) Act 1919 as limits the duration of that section, and section 5 of the Commonwealth Immigrants Act 1962 in so far as it limits the duration of Part I of that Act, shall cease to have effect on the passing of this Act.

Power to extend to Islands.

36.—Her Majesty may by Order in Council direct that any of the provisions of this Act shall extend, with such exceptions, adaptations and modifications, if any, as may be specified in the Order, to any of the Islands; and any Order in Council under this subsection may be varied or revoked by a further Order in Council.

Short title and extent.

37.—(1) This Act may be cited as the Immigration Act 1971.

(2) It is hereby declared that this Act extends to Northern Ireland, and (without prejudice to any provision of Schedule 1 to

this Act as to the extent of that Schedule) where an enactment repealed by this Act extends outside the United Kingdom, the repeal shall be of like extent.

SCHEDULES

[Schedule 1 was repealed by the British Nationality Act 1981.]

SCHEDULE 2
ADMINISTRATIVE PROVISIONS AS TO CONTROL ON ENTRY ETC.

PART I
GENERAL PROVISIONS

Immigration officers and medical inspectors

1.—(1) Immigration officers for the purposes of this Act shall be appointed by the Secretary of State, and he may arrange with the Commissioners of Customs and Excise for the employment of officers of customs and excise as immigration officers under this Act.

(2) Medical inspectors for the purposes of this Act may be appointed by the Secretary of State or, in Northern Ireland, by the Minister of Health and Social Services or other appropriate Minister of the Government of Northern Ireland in pursuance of arrangements made between that Minister and the Secretary of State, and shall be fully qualified medical practitioners.

(3) In the exercise of their functions under this Act immigration officers shall act in accordance with such instructions (not inconsistent with the immigration rules) as may be given them by the Secretary of State, and medical inspectors shall act in accordance with such instructions as may be given them by the Secretary of State or, in Northern Ireland, as may be given in pursuance of the arrangement mentioned in sub-paragraph (2) above by the Minister making appointments of medical inspectors in Northern Ireland.

(4) An immigration officer or medical inspector may board any ship or aircraft for the purpose of exercising his functions under this Act.

(5) An immigration officer, for the purpose of satisfying himself whether there are persons he may wish to examine under paragraph 2 below, may search any ship or aircraft and anything on board it, or any vehicle taken off a ship or aircraft on which it has been brought to the United Kingdom.

Examination by immigration officers, and medical examination

2.—(1) An immigration officer may examine any persons who have arrived in the United Kingdom by ship or aircraft (including transit passengers, members of the crew and others not seeking to enter the United Kingdom) for the purpose of determining—

(a) whether any of them is or is not a British citizen; and
(b) whether, if he is not, he may or may not enter the United Kingdom without leave; and
(c) whether, if he may not, he should be given leave and for what period and on what conditions (if any), or should be refused leave.

(2) Any such person, if he is seeking to enter the United Kingdom, may be examined also by a medical inspector or by any qualified person carrying out a test or examination required by a medical inspector.

(3) A person, on being examined under this paragraph by an immigration officer or medical inspector, may be required in writing by him to submit to further examination; but a requirement under this sub-paragraph shall not prevent a person who arrives as a transit passenger, or as a member of the crew of a ship or aircraft, or for the purpose of joining a ship or aircraft as a member of the crew, from leaving by his intended ship or aircraft.

3.—(1) An immigration officer may examine any person who is embarking or seeking to embark in the United Kingdom for the purpose of determining whether he is a British citizen, if he is not, for the purpose of establishing his identity.

(2) So long as any Order in Council is in force under section 3(7) of this Act, an immigration officer may examine any person who is embarking or seeking to embark in the United Kingdom for the purpose of determining—
(a) whether any of the provisions of the Order apply to him; and
(b) whether, if so, any power conferred by the Order should be exercised in relation to him and in what way.

Information and documents

4.—(1) It shall be the duty of any person examined under paragraph 2 or 3 above to furnish to the person carrying out the examination all such information in his possession as that person may require for the purpose of his functions under that paragraph.

(2) A person on his examination under paragraph 2 or 3 above by an immigration officer shall, if so required by the immigration officer—
(a) produce either a valid passport with photograph or some other document satisfactorily establishing his identity and nationality or citizenship; and
(b) declare whether or not he is carrying or conveying documents of any relevant description specified by the immigration officer, and produce any documents of that description which he is carrying or conveying.

In paragraph (b), "relevant description" means any description appearing to the immigration officer to be relevant for the purposes of the examination.

(3) Where under sub-paragraph (2)(b) above a person has been required to declare whether or not he is carrying or conveying documents of any description, he and any baggage belonging to him or under his control may be searched with a view to ascertaining whether he is doing so by the immigration officer or a person acting under the directions of the officer:

Provided that no woman or girl shall be searched except by a woman.

(4) An immigration officer may examine any documents produced pursuant to subparagraph (2)(b) above or found on a search under sub-paragraph (3), and may for that purpose detain them for any period not exceeding seven days; and if on examination of any documents so produced or found the immigration officer is of the opinion that it may be needed in connection with proceedings on an appeal under this Act or for an offence, he may detain it until he is satisfied that it will not be so needed.

5.—The Secretary of State may by order made by statutory instrument make provision for requiring passengers disembarking or embarking in the United Kingdom, or any class of passengers, to produce to an immigration officer, if so required, landing or embarkation cards in such form as the Secretary of State may direct, and for requiring the owners or agents of ships and aircraft to supply such cards to those passengers.

Notice of leave to enter or of refusal of leave

6.—(1) Subject to sub-paragraph (3) below, where a person examined by an immigration officer under paragraph 2 above is to be given a limited leave to enter the United Kingdom or is to be refused leave, the notice giving or refusing leave shall be given not later than twelve hours after the conclusion of his examination (including any further examination) in pursuance of that paragraph; and if notice giving or refusing leave is not given him before the end of those twelve hours, he shall (if not a British citizen) be deemed to have been given indefinite leave to enter the United Kingdom and the immigration officer shall as soon as may be give him written notice of that leave.

(2) Where on a person's examination under paragraph 2 above he is given notice of leave to enter the United Kingdom, then at any time before the end of twelve hours from the conclusion of the examination he may be given a further notice in writing by an immigration officer cancelling the earlier notice and refusing him leave to enter.

(3) Where in accordance with this paragraph a person is given notice refusing him leave to enter the United Kingdom, that notice may at any time be cancelled by notice in writing given him by an immigration officer; and where a person is given a notice of cancellation under this sub-paragraph, the immigration officer may at the same time give him a limited leave to enter, but in the absence of a notice giving a limited leave the notice of cancellation shall be deemed to be a notice giving him indefinite leave to enter.

(4) Where an entrant is a member of a party in charge of a person appearing to the immigration officer to be a responsible person, any notice to be given in relation to that entrant in accordance with this paragraph shall be duly given if delivered to the person in charge of the party.

Power to require medical examination after entry

7.—If, on a person's examination by an immigration officer under paragraph 2 above, the immigration officer—

(a) determines that he may be given leave to enter the United Kingdom; but
(b) is of opinion, on the advice of a medical inspector or, where no medical inspector is available, on that of any other fully qualified medical practitioner, that a further medical test or examination may be required in the interests of public health;

then the immigration officer, on giving that person leave to enter the United Kingdom, may by notice in writing require him to report his arrival to such medical officer of health or the chief administrative medical officer of such Health and Social Services Board established under the Health and Personal Social Services (Northern Ireland) Order 1972 as may be specified in the notice and thereafter to attend at such place and time, and submit to such test or examination (if any), as that medical officer may require.

Removal of persons refused leave to enter and illegal entrants

8.—(1) Where a person arriving in the United Kingdom is refused leave to enter, an immigration officer may, subject to sub-paragraph (2) below—
(a) give the captain of the ship or aircraft in which he arrives directions requiring the captain to remove him from the United Kingdom in that ship or aircraft; or
(b) give the owners or agents of that ship or aircraft directions requiring them to remove him from the United Kingdom in any ship or aircraft specified or indicated in the directions, being a ship or aircraft of which they are the owners or agents; or
(c) give those owners or agents directions requiring them to make arrangements for his removal from the United Kingdom in any ship or aircraft specified or indicated in the directions to a country or territory so specified, being either—
  (i) a country of which he is a national citizen; or
  (ii) a country or territory in which he has obtained a passport or other document of identity; or
  (iii) a country or territory in which he embarked for the United Kingdom; or
  (iv) a country or territory to which there is reason to believe that he will be admitted.

(2) No directions shall be given under this paragraph in respect of anyone after the expiration of two months beginning with the date on which he was refused leave to enter the United Kingdom.

9.—Where an illegal entrant is not given leave to enter or remain in the United Kingdom, an immigration officer may give any such directions in respect of him as in a case within paragraph 8 above are authorised by paragraph 8(1).

10.—(1) Where it appears to the Secretary of State either—
(a) that directions might be given in respect of a person under paragraph 8 or 9 above, but that it is not practicable for them to be given or that, if given, they would be ineffective; or

(b) that directions might have been given in respect of a person under paragraph 8 above but that the time limited by paragraph 8(2) has passed;

then the Secretary of State may give to the owners or agents of any ship or aircraft any such directions in respect of that person as are authorised by paragraph 8(1)(c).

(2) Where the Secretary of State may give directions for a person's removal in accordance with sub-paragraph (1) above, he may instead give directions for his removal in accordance with arrangements to be made by the Secretary of State to any country or territory to which he could be removed under subparagraph (1).

(3) The costs of complying with any directions given under this paragraph shall be defrayed by the Secretary of State.

11.—A person in respect of whom directions are given under any of paragraphs 8 to 10 above may be placed, under the authority of an immigration officer, on board any ship or aircraft in which he is to be removed in accordance with the directions.

Seamen and aircrews

12.—(1) If, on a person's examination by an immigration officer under paragraph 2 above, the immigration officer is satisfied that he has come to the United Kingdom for the purpose of joining a ship or aircraft as a member of the crew, then the immigration officer may limit the duration of any leave he gives that person to enter the United Kingdom by requiring him to leave the United Kingdom in a ship or aircraft specified or indicated by the notice giving leave.

(2) Where a person (not being a British citizen) arrives in the United Kingdom for the purpose of joining a ship or aircraft as a member of the crew and, having been given leave to enter as mentioned in sub-paragraph (1) above, remains beyond the time limited by that leave, or is reasonably suspected by an immigration officer of intending to do so, an immigration officer may—

(a) give the captain of that ship or aircraft directions requiring the captain to remove him from the United Kingdom in that ship or aircraft; or

(b) give the owners or agents of that ship or aircraft directions requiring them to remove him from the United Kingdom in any ship or aircraft specified or indicated in the directions, being a ship or aircraft of which they are the owners or agents; or

(c) give those owners or agents directions requiring them to make arrangements for his removal from the United Kingdom in any ship or aircraft specified or indicated in the directions to a country or territory so specified, being either—
   (i) a country of which he is a national or citizen; or
   (ii) a country or territory in which he has obtained a passport or other documents of identity; or

(iii) a country or territory in which he embarked for the United Kingdom; or
(iv) a country or territory where he was engaged as a member of the crew of the ship or aircraft which he arrived in the United Kingdom to join; or
(v) a country or territory to which there is reason to believe that he will be admitted.

13.—(1) Where a person being a member of the crew of a ship or aircraft is examined by an immigration officer under paragraph 2 above, the immigration officer may limit the duration of any leave he gives that person to enter the United Kingdom—
(a) in the manner authorised by paragraph 12(1) above; or
(b) if that person is to be allowed to enter the United Kingdom in order to receive hospital treatment, by requiring him, on completion of that treatment, to leave the United Kingdom in accordance with arrangements to be made for his repatriation; or
(c) by requiring him to leave the United Kingdom within a specified period in accordance with arrangements to be made for his repatriation.
(2) Where a person (not being a British citizen) arrives in the United Kingdom as a member of the crew of a ship or aircraft, and either—
(A) having lawfully entered the United Kingdom without leave by virtue of section 8(1) of this Act, he remains without leave beyond the time allowed by section 8(1), or is reasonably suspected by an immigration officer of intending to do so; or
(B) having been given leave limited as mentioned in subparagraph (1) above, he remains beyond the time limited by that leave, or is reasonably suspected by an immigration officer of intending to do so;
an immigration officer may—
(a) give the captain of the ship or aircraft in which he arrived directions requiring the captain to remove him from the United Kingdom in that ship or aircraft; or
(b) give the owners or agents of that ship or aircraft directions requiring them to remove him from the United Kingdom in any ship or aircraft specified or indicated in the directions, being a ship or aircraft of which they are the owners or agents; or
(c) give those owners or agents directions requiring them to make arrangements for his removal from the United Kingdom in any ship or aircraft specified or indicated in the directions to a country or territory so specified, being either—
    (i) a country in which he is a national citizen; or
    (ii) a country or territory in which he has obtained a passport or other document of identity; or
    (iii) a country in which he embarked for the United Kingdom; or
    (iv) a country or territory in which he was engaged as a member of the

crew of the ship or aircraft in which he arrived in the United Kingdom; or

(v) a country or territory to which there is reason to believe that he will be admitted.

14.—(1) Where it appears to the Secretary of State that directions might be given in respect of a person under paragraph 12 or 13 above, but that it is not practicable for them to be given or that, if given, they would be ineffective, then the Secretary of State may give to the owners or agents of any ship or aircraft any such directions in respect of that person as are authorised by paragraph 12(2)(c) or 13(2)(c).

(2) Where the Secretary of State may give directions for a person's removal in accordance with sub-paragraph (1) above, he may instead give directions for his removal in accordance with arrangements to be made by the Secretary of State to any country or territory to which he could be removed under subparagraph (1).

(3) The costs of complying with any directions given under this paragraph shall be defrayed by the Secretary of State.

15.—A person in respect of whom directions are given under any of paragraphs 12 to 14 above may be placed, under the authority of an immigration officer, on board any ship or aircraft in which he is to be removed in accordance with the directions.

Detention of persons liable to examination or removal

16.—(1) A person who may be required to submit to examination under paragraph 2 above may be detained under the authority of an immigration officer pending his examination and pending a decision to give or refuse him leave to enter.

(2) A person in respect of whom directions may be given under any of paragraphs 8 to 14 above may be detained under the authority of an immigration officer pending the giving of directions and pending his removal in pursuance of any directions given.

(3) A person on board a ship or aircraft may, under the authority of an immigration officer, be removed from the ship or aircraft for detention under this paragraph; but if an immigration officer so requires the captain of a ship or aircraft shall prevent from disembarking in the United Kingdom any person who has arrived in the United Kingdom in the ship or aircraft and been refused leave to enter, and the captain may for that purpose detain him in custody on board the ship or aircraft.

(4) The captain of a ship or aircraft, if so required by an immigration officer, shall prevent from disembarking in the United Kingdom or before the directions for his removal have been fulfilled any person placed on board the ship or aircraft under paragraph 11 or 15 above, and the captain may for that purpose detain him in custody on board the ship or aircraft.

17.—(1) A person liable to be detained under paragraph 16 above may be arrested without warrant by a constable or by an immigration officer.

(2) If—

(a) a justice of the peace is by written information on oath satisfied that there is reasonable ground for suspecting that a person liable to be arrested under this paragraph is to be found on any premises; or

(b) in Scotland, a sheriff, or a magistrate or justice of the peace, having jurisdiction in the place where the premises are situated is by evidence on oath so satisfied;

he may grant a warrant authorising any constable acting for the police area in which the premises are situated, or in Northern Ireland any constable, at any time or times within one month from the date of the warrant to enter, if need be by force, the premises named in the warrant for the purpose of searching for and arresting that person.

18.—(1) Persons may be detained under paragraph 16 above in such places as the Secretary of State may direct (when not detained in accordance with paragraph 16 on board a ship or aircraft).

(2) Where a person is detained under paragraph 16, any immigration officer, constable or prison officer, or any other person authorised by the Secretary of State, may take all such steps as may be reasonably necessary for photographing, measuring or otherwise identifying him.

(3) Any person detained under paragraph 16 may be taken in the custody of a constable, or of any person acting under the authority of an immigration officer, to and from any place where his attendance is required for the purpose of ascertaining his citizenship or nationality or of making arrangements for his admission to a country or territory other than the United Kingdom, or where he is required to be for any other purpose connected with the operation of this Act.

(4) A person shall be deemed to be in legal custody at any time when he is detained under paragraph 16 or is being removed in pursuance of subparagraph (3) above.

19.—(1) Where a person is refused leave to enter the United Kingdom and directions are given in respect of him under paragraphs 8 or 10 above, then subject to the provisions of this paragraph the owners or agents of the ship or aircraft in which he arrived shall be liable to pay the Secretary of State on demand any expenses incurred by the latter in respect of the custody, accommodation or maintenance of that person at any time after his arrival while he was detained or liable to be detained under paragraph 16 above.

(2) Sub-paragraph (1) above shall not apply to expenses in respect of a person who, when he arrived in the United Kingdom, held a certificate of entitlement, or a current entry clearance or was the person named in a current work permit; and for this purpose a document purporting to be a certificate of entitlement, entry clearance or work permit is to be regarded as being one unless its falsity is reasonably apparent.

(3) If, before the directions for a person's removal under paragraph 8 or 10 above have been carried out, he is given leave to enter the United Kingdom, or if he is afterwards given that leave in consequence of the determination in his favour of an appeal under this Act (being an appeal against a refusal of leave to enter by virtue of which the directions were given), or it is determined on an appeal under this Act that he does not require leave to enter (being an appeal occasioned by such a refusal), no sum shall be demanded under sub-paragraph (1) above for expenses incurred in respect of that person and any sum already demanded and paid shall be refunded.

(4) Sub-paragraph (1) above shall not have effect in relation to directions which, in consequence of an appeal under this Act, have ceased to have effect or are for the time being of no effect; and the expenses to which that subparagraph applies include expenses in conveying the person in question to and from the place where he is detained or accommodated unless the journey is made for the purpose of attending an appeal by him under this Act.

20.—(1) Subject to the provisions of this paragraph, in either of the following cases, that is to say,—

(a) where directions are given in respect of an illegal entrant under paragraph 9 or 10 above; and

(b) where a person has lawfully entered the United Kingdom without leave by virtue of section 8(1) of this Act, but directions are given in respect of him under paragraph 13(2)(A) above or, in a case within paragraph 13(2)(A), under paragraph 14;

the owners or agents of the ship or aircraft in which he arrived in the United Kingdom shall be liable to pay the Secretary of State on demand any expenses incurred by the latter in respect of the custody, accommodation or maintenance of that person at any time after his arrival while he was detained or liable to be detained under paragraph 16 above.

(2) If, before the directions for a person's removal from the United Kingdom have been carried out, he is given leave to remain in the United Kingdom, no sum shall be demanded under sub-paragraph (1) above for expenses incurred in respect of that person and any sum already demanded and paid shall be refunded.

(3) Sub-paragraph (1) above shall not have effect in relation to directions which, in consequence of an appeal under this Act, are for the time being of no effect; and the expenses to which that sub-paragraph applies include expenses in conveying the person in question to and from the place where he is detained or accommodated unless the journey is made for the purpose of attending an appeal by him under this Act.

Temporary admission or release of persons liable to detention

21.—(1) A person liable to detention or detained under paragraph 16 above may, under the written authority of an immigration officer, be temporarily admitted to the United Kingdom without being detained or be released from detention; but this shall not prejudice a later exercise of the power to detain him.

(2) So long as a person is at large in the United Kingdom by virtue of this paragraph, he shall be subject to such restrictions as to residence and as to reporting to the police or an immigration officer as may from time to time be notifed to him in writing by an immigration officer.

22.—(1) A person detained under paragraph 16(1) above pending examination may, if seven days have elapsed since the date of his arrival in the United Kingdom, be released on bail by an adjudicator on his entering into a recognizance or, in Scotland, bail bond conditioned for his appearance before an immigration officer at a time and place named in the recognizance or bail bond or at such other time or place as may in the meantime be notified to him in writing by an immigration officer.

(2) The conditions of a recognizance or bail bond taken under this paragraph may include conditions appearing to the adjudicator to be likely to result in the appearance of the person bailed at the required time and place; and any recognizance shall be with or without sureties as the adjudicator may determine.

(3) In any case in which an adjudicator has power under this paragraph to release a person on bail, the adjudicator may, instead of taking the bail, fix the amount and conditions of the bail (including the amount in which any sureties are to be bound) with a view to its being taken subsequently by any such person as may be specified by the adjudicator; and on the recognizance or bail bond being so taken the person to be bailed should be released.

23.—(1) Where a recognizance entered into under paragraph 22 above appears to an adjudicator to be forfeited, the adjudicator may by order declare it to be forfeited and adjudge the persons bound thereby, whether as principal or sureties, or any of them, to pay the sum in which they are respectively bound or such part of it, if any, as the adjudicator thinks fit; and an order under this sub-paragraph shall specify a magistrates' court or, in Northern Ireland, court of summary jurisdiction, and—

(a) the recognizance shall be treated for the purposes of collection, enforcement and remission of the sum forfeited as having been forfeited by the court so specified; and

(b) the adjudicator shall, as soon as practicable, give particulars of the recognizance to the clerk of that court.

(2) Where a person released on bail under paragraph 22 above as it applies in Scotland fails to comply with the terms of his bail bond, an adjudicator may declare the bail to be forfeited, and any bail so forfeited shall be transmitted by the adjudicator to the sheriff court having jurisdiction in the area where the proceedings took place, and shall be treated as having been forfeited by that court.

(3) Any sum the payment of which is enforceable by a magistrates' court in England or Wales by virtue of this paragraph shall be treated for the purposes

of the Justices of the Peace Act 1979 and, in particular, section 61 thereof as being due under a recognizance forfeited by such a court.

(4) Any sum the payment of which is enforceable by virtue of this paragraph by a court of summary jurisdiction in Northern Ireland shall, for the purposes of section 20(5) of the Administration of Justice Act (Northern Ireland) 1954, be treated as a forfeited recognizance.

24.—(1) An immigration officer or constable may arrest without warrant a person who has been released by virtue of paragraph 22 above—

(a) if he has reasonable grounds for believing that that person is likely to break the condition of his recognizance or bail bond that he will appear at the time and place required or to break any other condition of it, or has reasonable ground to suspect that that person is breaking or has broken any such other condition; or

(b) if, a recognizance with sureties having been taken, he is notified in writing by any surety of the surety's belief that that person is likely to break the first-mentioned condition, and of the surety's wish for that reason to be relieved of his obligations as a surety;

and paragraph 17(2) above shall apply for the arrest of a person under this paragraph as it applies for the arrest of a person under paragraph 17.

(2) A person arrested under this paragraph—

(a) if not required by a condition on which he was released to appear before an immigration officer within twenty-four fours after the time of his arrest, shall as soon as practicable be brought before an adjudicator or, if that is not practicable within those twenty-four hours, before a justice of the peace acting for the petty sessions area in which he is arrested or, in Scotland, the sheriff; and

(b) if required by such a condition to appear within those twenty-four hours before an immigration officer, shall be brought before that officer.

(3) An adjudicator, justice of the peace or sheriff before whom a person is brought by virtue of sub-paragraph (2)(a) above—

(a) if of the opinion that that person has broken or is likely to break any condition on which he was released, may either—

  (i) direct that he be detained under the authority of the person by whom he was arrested; or

  (ii) release him, on his original recognizance or on a new recognizance, with or without sureties, or, in Scotland, on his original bail or on new bail; and

(b) if not of that opinion, shall release him on his original recognizance or bail.

25.—The power to make rules of procedure conferred by section 22 of this Act shall include power to make rules with respect to applications to an adjudicator under paragraphs 22 to 24 above and matters arising out of such applications.

Supplementary duties of those connected with ships or aircraft or with ports

26.—(1) The owners or agents of a ship or aircraft employed to carry passengers for reward shall not, without the approval of the Secretary of State, arrange for the ship or aircraft to call at a port in the United Kingdom other than a port of entry for the purpose of disembarking passengers, if any of the passengers on board may not enter the United Kingdom without leave and have not been given leave, or for the purpose of embarking passengers unless the owners or agents have reasonable cause to believe all of them to be British citizens.

(2) The Secretary of State may from time to time give written notice to the owners or agents of any ships or aircraft designating control areas for the embarkation or disembarkation of passengers in any port in the United Kingdom, and specifying the conditions and restrictions (if any) to be observed in any control area; and where by notice given to any owners or agents a control area is for the time being designated for the embarkation or disembarkation of passengers at any port, the owners or agents shall take all reasonable steps to secure that, in the case of their ships or aircraft, passengers do not embark or disembark, as the case may be, at the port outside the control area and that any conditions or restrictions notifed to them are observed.

(3) The Secretary of State may also from time to time give to any person concerned with the management of a port in the United Kingdom written notice designating control areas in the port and specifying conditions or restrictions to be observed in any control area; and any such person shall take all reasonable steps to secure that any conditions or restrictions as notified to him are observed.

27.—(1) The captain of a ship or aircraft arriving in the United Kingdom—

(a) shall take such steps as may be necessary to secure that persons on board do not disembark there unless either they have been examined by an immigration officer, or they disembark in accordance with arrangements approved by an immigration officer, or they are members of the crew who may lawfully enter the United Kingdom without leave by virtue of section 8(1) of this Act; and

(b) where the examination of persons on board is to be carried out on the ship or aircraft, shall take such steps as may be necessary to secure that those to be examined are presented for the purpose in an orderly manner.

(2) The Secretary of State may by order made by statutory instrument make provision for requiring captains of ships or aircraft arriving in the United Kingdom, or of such of them as arrive from or by way of countries or places specified in the order, to furnish to immigration officers—

(a) a passenger list showing the names and nationality or citizenship of passengers arriving on board the ship or aircraft;

(b) particulars of members of the crew of the ship or aircraft;

and for enabling an immigration officer to dispense with the furnishing of any such list or particulars.

PART II

EFFECT OF APPEALS

Stay on directions for removal

28.—(1) Where a person in the United Kingdom appeals under section 13(1) of this Act on being refused leave to enter, any directions previously given by virtue of the refusal for his removal from the United Kingdom shall cease to have effect, except in so far as they have already been carried out, and no directions shall be so given so long as the appeal is pending.

(2) Where a person in the United Kingdom appeals under section 16 or 17 of this Act against any directions given under Part I of this Schedule for his removal from the United Kingdom, those directions, except in so far as they have already been carried out, shall be of no effect so long as the appeal is pending.

(3) Notwithstanding sub-paragraph (1) or (2) above, the provisions of Part I of this Schedule with respect to detention and persons liable to detention shall apply to a person appealing under section 13(1), 16 or 17 of this Act as if there were in force directions for his removal from the United Kingdom, except that he shall not be detained on board a ship or aircraft so as to compel him to leave the United Kingdom while the appeal is pending.

(4) In calculating the period of two months limited by paragraph 8(2) above for the giving of directions under that paragraph for the removal of a person from the United Kingdom, there shall be disregarded any period during which there is pending an appeal by him under section 13(1) or 17 of this Act.

(5) For purposes of sub-paragraphs (1) to (3) above (but not for purposes of sub-paragraph (4)), where an appeal to an adjudicator is dismissed, an appeal shall not be regarded as pending unless forthwith after the dismissal—

(a) the appellant duly gives notice of appeal against the determination of the adjudicator; or

(b) in a case in which leave to appeal against that determination is required and the adjudicator has power to grant leave, the appellant duly applies for and obtains the leave of the adjudicator.

(6) Where directions are given under Part I of this Schedule for anyone's removal from the United Kingdom, and directions are also so given for the removal with him of persons belonging to his family, then if any of them appeals under section 13(1), 16 or 17 of this Act, the appeal shall have the like effect under this paragraph in relation to the directions given in respect of each of the others as it has in relation to the directions given in respect of the appellant.

Grant of bail pending appeal

29.—(1) Where a person (in the following provisions of this Schedule referred to as 'an appellant') has an appeal pending under section 13(1), 16 or 17 of this Act and is for the time being detained under Part I of this Schedule, he may be released on bail in accordance with this paragraph.

(2) An immigration officer not below the rank of chief immigration officer or a police officer not below the rank of inspector may release an appellant on his entering into a recognizance or, in Scotland, bail bond conditioned for his appearance before an adjudicator or the Appeal Tribunal at a time and place named in the recognizance or bail bond.

(3) An adjudicator may release an appellant on his entering into a recognizance or, in Scotland, bail bond conditioned for his appearance before that or any other adjudicator or the Appeal Tribunal at a time and place named in the recognizance or bail bond; and where an adjudicator dismisses an appeal but grants leave to the appellant to appeal to the Tribunal, or, in a case in which leave to appeal is not required, the appellant has duly given notice of appeal to the Tribunal, the adjudicator shall, if the appellant so requests, exercise his powers under this sub-paragraph.

(4) Where an appellant has duly applied for leave to appeal to the Appeal Tribunal, the Tribunal may release him on his entering into a recognizance or, in Scotland, bail bond conditioned for his appearance before the Tribunal at a time and place named in the recognizance or bail bond; and where—

(a) the Tribunal grants leave to an appellant to appeal to the Tribunal; or

(b) in a case in which leave to appeal is not required, the appellant has duly given notice of appeal to the Tribunal;

the Tribunal shall, if the appellant so requests, release him as aforesaid.

(5) The conditions of a recognizance or bail bond taken under this paragraph may include conditions appearing to the person fixing the bail to be likely to result in the appearance of the appellant at the time and place named; and any recognizance shall be with or without sureties as that person may determine.

(6) In any case in which an adjudicator or the Tribunal has power or is required by this paragraph to release an appellant on bail, the adjudicator or Tribunal may, instead of taking the bail, fix the amount and conditions of the bail (including the amount in which any sureties are to be bound) with a view to its being taken subsequently by any such person as may be specified by the adjudicator or the Tribunal; and on the recognizance or bail bond being so taken the appellant shall be released.

Restrictions on grant of bail

30.—(1) An appellant shall not be released under paragraph 29 above without the consent of the Secretary of State if directions for the removal of the appellant from the United Kingdom are for the time being in force, or the power to give such directions is for the time being exercisable.

(2) Notwithstanding paragraph 29(3) or (4) above, an adjudicator and the Tribunal shall not be obliged to release an appellant unless the appellant enters into a proper recognizance, with sufficient and satisfactory sureties if required, or in Scotland sufficient and satisfactory bail is found if so required; and an adjudicator and the Tribunal shall not be obliged to release an appellant if it appears to the adjudicator or the Tribunal, as the case may be—

(a) that the appellant, having on any previous occasion been released on bail (whether under paragraph 24 or under any other provision), has failed to comply with the conditions of any recognizance or bail bond entered into by him on that occasion;

(b) that the appellant is likely to commit an offence unless he is retained in detention;

(c) that the release of the appellant is likely to cause danger to public health;

(d) that the appellant is suffering from mental disorder and that his continued detention is necessary in his own interests or for the protection of any other person; or

(e) that the appellant is under the age of seventeen, that arrangements ought to be made for his care in the event of his release and that no satisfactory arrangements for that purpose have been made.

Forfeiture of recognizances

31.—(1) Where under paragraph 29 above (as it applies in England and Wales or in Northern Ireland) a recognizance is entered into conditioned for the appearance of an appellant before an adjudicator or the Tribunal, and it appears to the adjudicator or the Tribunal, as the case may be, to be forfeited, the adjudicator or Tribunal may by order declare it to be forfeited and adjudge the persons bound thereby, whether as principal or sureties, or any of them, to pay the sum in which they are respectively bound or such part of it, if any, as the adjudicator or Tribunal thinks fit.

(2) An order under this paragraph shall, for the purposes of this sub-paragraph, specify a magistrates' court or, in Northern Ireland, court of summary jurisdiction; and the recognizance shall be treated for the purposes of collection, enforcement and remission of the sum forfeited as having been forfeited by the court so specified.

(3) Where an adjudicator or the Tribunal makes an order under this paragraph the adjudicator or Tribunal shall, as soon as practicable, give particulars of the recognizance to the clerk of the court specified in the order in pursuance of sub-paragraph (2) above.

(4) Any sum the payment of which is enforceable by a magistrates' court in England or Wales by virtue of this paragraph shall be treated for the purposes of the Justices of the Peace Act 1979 and, in particular, section 61 thereof as being due under a recognizance forfeited by such a court.

(5) Any sum the payment of which is enforceable by virtue of this paragraph by a court of summary jurisdiction in Northern Ireland shall, for the purposes of section 20(5) of the Administration of Justice Act (Northern Ireland) 1954, be treated as a forfeited recognizance.

32.—Where under paragraph 29 above (as it applies in Scotland) a person released on bail fails to comply with the terms of a bail bond conditioned for his appearance before an adjudicator or the Tribunal, the adjudicator or Tribunal may declare the bail to be forfeited, and any bail so forfeited shall be transmitted by the adjudicator or the Tribunal to the sheriff court having jurisdiction in the area where the proceedings took place, and shall be treated as having been forfeited by that court.

Arrest of appellants released on bail

33.—(1) An immigration officer or constable may arrest without warrant a person who has been released by virtue of this Part of this Schedule—

(a) if he has reasonable grounds for believing that that person is likely to break the condition of his recognizance or bail bond that he will appear at the time and place required or to break any other condition of it, or has reasonable ground to suspect that that person is breaking or has broken any such other condition; or

(b) if, a recognizance with sureties having been taken, he is notified in writing by any surety of the surety's belief that that person is likely to break the first-mentioned condition, and of the surety's wish for that reason to be relieved of his obligations as a surety;

and paragraph 17(2) above shall apply for the arrest of a person under this paragraph as it applies for the arrest of a person under paragraph 17.

(2) A person arrested under this paragraph—

(a) if not required by a condition on which he was released to appear before an adjudicator or Tribunal within twenty-four hours after the time of his arrest, shall as soon as practicable be brought before an adjudicator or, if that is not practicable within those twenty-four hours, before a justice of the peace acting for the petty sessions area in which he is arrested or, in Scotland, the sheriff; and

(b) if required by such a condition to appear within those twenty-four hours before an adjudicator or before the Tribunal, shall be brought before that adjudicator or before the Tribunal, as the case may be.

(3) An adjudicator, justice of the peace or sheriff before whom a person is brought by virtue of sub-paragraph (2)(a) above—

(a) if of the opinion that that person has broken or is likely to break any condition on which he was released, may either—

(i) direct that he be detained under the authority of the person by whom he was arrested; or

(ii) release him on his original recognizance or on a new recognizance, with or without sureties, or, in Scotland, on his original bail or on new bail; and

(b) if not of that opinion, shall release him on his original recognizance or bail.

SCHEDULE 3

SUPPLEMENTARY PROVISIONS AS TO DEPORTATION

Removal of persons liable to deportation

1.—(1) Where a deportation order is in force against any person, the Secretary of State may give directions for his removal to a country or territory specified in the directions being either—

(a) a country of which he is a national or citizen; or

(b) a country or territory to which there is reason to believe that he will be admitted.

(2) The directions under sub-paragraph (1) above may be either—

(a) directions given to the captain of a ship or aircraft about to leave the United Kingdom requiring him to remove the person in question in that ship or aircraft; or

(b) directions given to the owners or agents of any ship or aircraft requiring them to make arrangements for his removal in a ship or aircraft specified or indicated in the directions; or

(c) directions for his removal in accordance with arrangements to be made by the Secretary of State.

(3) In relation to directions given under this paragraph, paragraphs 11 and 16(4) of Schedule 2 to this Act shall apply, with the substitution of references to the secretary of State for references to an immigration officer, as they apply in relation to directions for removal given under paragraph 8 of that Schedule.

(4) The Secretary of State, if he thinks fit, may apply in or towards payment of the expenses of or incidental to the voyage from the United Kingdom of a person against whom a deportation order is in force, or the maintenance until departure of such a person and his dependants, if any, any money belonging to that person; and except so far as they are paid as aforesaid, those expenses shall be defrayed by the Secretary of State.

Detention or control pending deportation

2.—(1) Where a recommendation for deportation made by a court is in force in respect of any person, and that person is neither detained in pursuance of the sentence or order of any court nor for the time being released on bail by any court having power so to release him, he shall, unless the court by which the recommendation is made otherwise directs, or a direction is given under sub-paragraph (1A) below, be detained pending the making of a deportation order in pursuance of the recommendation, unless the Secretary of State directs him to be released pending further consideration of his case.

(1A) Where—

(a) a recommendation for deportation made by a court on conviction of a person is in force in respect of him; and

(b) he appeals against his conviction or against that recommendation,

the powers that the court determining the appeal may exercise include power to direct him to be released without setting aside the recommendation.

(2) Where notice has been given to a person in accordance with regulations under section 18 of this Act of a decision to make a deportation order against him, and he is neither detained in pursuance of the sentence or order of a court nor for the time being released on bail by a court having power to so release him, he may be detained under the authority of the Secretary of State pending the making of the deportation order.

(3) Where a deportation order is in force against any person, he may be

detained under the authority of the Secretary of State pending his removal or departure from the United Kingdom (and if already detained by virtue of sub-paragraph (1) or (2) above when the order is made, shall continue to be detained unless the Secretary of State directs otherwise).

(4) In relation to detention under sub-paragraph (2) or (3) above, paragraphs 17 and 18 of Schedule 2 to this Act shall apply as they apply in relation to detention under paragraph 16 of that Schedule.

(5) A person to whom this sub-paragraph applies shall be subject to such restrictions as to residence and as to reporting to the police as may from time to time be notified to him in writing by the Secretary of State.

(6) The persons to whom sub-paragraph (5) above applies are—

(a) a person liable to be detained under sub-paragraph (1) above, while by virtue of a direction of the Secretary of State he is not so detained; and

(b) a person liable to be detained under sub-paragraph (2) or (3) above, while he is not so detained.

Effect of appeals

3.—Part II of Schedule 2 to this Act, so far as it relates to appeals under section 16 or 17, shall apply for purposes of this Schedule as if the references in paragraph 28(2), (3) and (6) and in paragraph 29(1) to Part I of that Schedule were references to this Schedule; and paragraphs 29 to 33 shall apply in like manner in relation to appeals under section 15(1)(a).

Powers of courts pending deportation

4.—Where the release of a person recommended for deportation is directed by a court, he shall be subject to such restrictions as to residence and as to reporting to the police as the court may direct.

5.—(1) On an application made—

(a) by or on behalf of a person recommended for deportation whose release was so directed; or

(b) by a constable; or

(c) by an immigration officer,

the appropriate court shall have the powers specified in sub-paragraph (2) below.

(2) The powers mentioned in sub-paragraph (1) above are—

(a) if the person to whom the application relates is not subject to any such restrictions imposed by a court as are mentioned in paragraph 4 above, to order that he shall be subject to any such restrictions as the court may direct; and

(b) if he is subject to such restrictions imposed by a court by virtue of that paragraph or this paragraph—

(i) to direct that any of them shall be varied or shall cease to have effect; or

(ii) to give further directions as to his residence and reporting.

6.—(1) In this Schedule "the appropriate court" means, except in a case to which sub-paragraph (2) below applies, the court which directed release.

(2) This sub-paragraph applies where the court which directed release was—

(a) the Crown Court;
(b) the Court of Appeal;
(c) the High Court of Justiciary;
(d) the Crown Court in Northern Ireland; or
(e) the Court of Appeal in Northern Ireland.

(3) Where the Crown Court or the Crown Court in Northern Ireland directed release, the appropriate court is—

(a) the court that directed release; or
(b) a magistrates' court acting for the commission area or county court division where the person to whom the application relates resides.

(4) Where the Court of Appeal or the Court of Appeal in Northern Ireland gave the direction, the appropriate court is the Crown Court or the Crown Court in Northern Ireland, as the case may be.

(5) Where the High Court of Justiciary directed release, the appropriate court is—

(a) that court; or
(b) in a case where release was directed by that court on appeal, the court from which the appeal was made.

7.—(1) A constable or immigration officer may arrest without warrant any person who is subject to restrictions imposed by a court under this Schedule and who at the time of the arrest is in the relevant part of the United Kingdom—

(a) if he has reasonable grounds to suspect that that person is contravening or has contravened any of those restrictions; or
(b) if he has reasonable grounds for believing that that person is likely to contravene any of them.

(2) In sub-paragraph (1) above "the relevant part of the United Kingdom" means—

(a) England and Wales, in a case where a court with jurisdiction in England or Wales imposed the restrictions;
(b) Scotland, in a case where a court with jurisdiction in Scotland imposed them; and
(c) Northern Ireland, in a case where a court in Northern Ireland imposed them.

8.—(1) A person arrested in England or Wales or Northern Ireland in pursuance of paragraph 7 above shall be brought as soon as practicable and in any event within 24 hours after his arrest before a justice of the peace for the petty sessions area or district in which he was arrested.

(2) In reckoning for the purposes of this paragraph any period of 24 hours, no account shall be taken of Christmas Day, Good Friday or any Sunday.

9.—(1) A person arrested in Scotland in pursuance of paragraph 7 above shall wherever practicable be brought before the appropriate court not later than in the course of the first day after his arrest, such day not being a Saturday, a Sunday or a court holiday prescribed for that court under section 10 of the Bail etc. (Scotland) Act 1980.

(2) Nothing in this paragraph shall prevent a person arrested in Scotland being brought before a court on a Saturday, a Sunday or such a court holiday as is mentioned in sub-paragraph (1) above where the court is, in pursuance of section 10 of the said Act of 1980, sitting on such day for the disposal of criminal business.

10.—Any justice of the peace or court before whom a person is brought by virtue of paragraph 8 or 9 above—

(a) if of the opinion that that person is contravening, has contravened or is likely to contravene any restriction imposed on him by a court under this Schedule, may direct—
 (i) that he be detained; or
 (ii) that he be released subject to such restrictions as to his residence and reporting to the police as the court may direct; and

(b) if not of that opinion, shall release him without altering the restrictions as to his residence and his reporting to the police.

Note: Schs 4–6 for present purposes are unimportant, and accordingly are not reproduced here.

Index

REMEDIES FOR VICTIMS OF CRIME

by Suzanne Bailey and David Tucker

This Guide is designed for those advising individuals, who have been the victim of a crime, of their rights to financial compensation. Relevant cases and other legal sources have been included for legal practitioners.

The starting point is the crime/remedy table which lists various offences and shows possible sources of compensation for victims, depending on whether a suspect has been traced or convicted. Potential sources of compensation are dealt with in succeeding chapters.

"a welcome addition" — *Social Work Today*

£5.00 including postage (published November 1984).

LEGAL AID — HOW TO USE IT

by Ole Hansen with Howard Levenson

A practical Guide to and a commentary on the legal aid legislation and regulations. It should be used in conjunction with the Law Society's *Legal Aid Handbook.*

In his introduction, Ole Hansen stresses that:

"we intend to explain how to make the scheme work to the best advantage of consumers and (the objective is not necessarily incompatible) to the best advantage of lawyers."

The range of help available under both the civil and criminal legal aid schemes is explained in detail.

Separate chapters are devoted to the green form scheme, assistance by way of representation, the civil legal aid certificate, emergency applications, legal aid in family proceedings, the conduct of legally-aided litigation, costs, the statutory charge and the new criminal legal aid scheme.

£11.00 including postage (published October 1985).

All titles available from LAG, 242-244 Pentonville Road, London N1 9UN.

Please send cash with orders, making cheques payable to: Legal Action Group.